MW01028741

My Quarter-Life Crisis

How an Anxiety Disorder
Knocked Me Down,
and How I Got Back Up

By
Lee Wellman

Letter from the Author

I never aspired to be an author. I am not a professional therapist, a PhD, or even an established writer—just your typical, everyday guy. I am an athlete by nature, a salesman by trade, an MBA by degree, yet an author by opportunity, for I had a story to share. I wrote this book to help others. My surprising and debilitating experiences with anxiety and panic burdened me with a sense of responsibility to share my compelling story with the sole hope of helping people.

I've received hundreds of testimonies and praises that my story, my candid experiences, and my advice—specifically *The Cheat Sheet* (Chapter 10)—have positively impacted my readers. After all, I am an anxiety survivor, a recovered sufferer if you will.

My book has been endorsed by countless therapists and psychiatrists and in fact has become one of the most recommended books to patients suffering from anxiety and/or panic in the Boston area.

With that said, I thank you for your interest in <u>My Quarter-Life Crisis</u>. I wish you well in your journey and hope you can take something beneficial and purposeful away from my story.

Best Wishes,

Lee Wellman

This book is dedicated to all that played a part in helping me conquer my anxiety disorder:

Katie—my love and my editor,
Janet Fronk—APRN Clinical Specialist,
my parents, sisters, and grandparents,
Kara, Nicole, and all of my other close friends

Friends and family are the angels who lift us to our feet when our wings have trouble remembering how to fly.

- Anonymous

www.leewellman.com

ISBN 0-9787515-7-4

ISBN 978-0-9787515-7-9

Tucket Publishing, LLC. – 2007
P.O. Box E – 44
Boston, MA 02127
www.leewellman.com

Table of Contents

Foreword

I want to share with you a story about how an anxiety disorder turned my life upside down—how anxiety, fear, and panic knocked me down and changed my life within the matter of one day. This was not typical, everyday anxiety that is healthy and natural, nor was it situational anxiety that comes and goes based on stressful events and circumstances. This was constant and uncontrollable anxiety that ruled every second of every day. This anxiety—my anxiety—had truly become a disorder. I want to tell you about my struggle with anxiety and the skills that I developed to help me overcome my harmful thoughts and feelings. I believe my story will equip you with the knowledge and awareness necessary to handle your thoughts and feelings and hopefully avoid an anxiety disorder altogether.

My struggle with anxiety was amplified in large part because I knew very little about the condition and its potentially disastrous effects. I knew nothing about the symptoms, effects, or dangers associated with the disorder. I was oblivious to the fact that anxiety can very quickly convince you that you can't handle life's adversities and challenges, large or small. My ignorance led to a much longer and more tumultuous battle with anxiety as I allowed it to completely infiltrate every aspect of my life. If I was equipped then with the knowledge about anxiety that I possess today, I believe I could have better controlled my anxious feelings and prevented them from developing into a disorder. Knowledge is power. Informing unsuspecting victims about anxiety and its related disorders is the first step in prevention.

This book will resonate with those of you who consider yourselves to be motivated and driven people, constantly striving for success and achievement in all aspects of your life. Contrary to popular belief, it is you who are typically the people most affected by anxiety. Anxiety is actually a natural part of all of us as human beings. It can be a very positive tool because it is what drives us to push ourselves to succeed. I like to say it is what keeps us off our couches all day long. Yet, when anxiety becomes abnormal or excessive, it can quickly become a very negative force. It is only our knowledge, skills, and our ability to control this anxiety that can allow us to maintain its positive effects. But for many of us, the ability to control anxiety does not come naturally. These skills must be taught, learned, retained, and practiced. Finding a source that provides helpful strategies for controlling anxiety is not very easy.

For me, speaking with my friends and family who had had similar experiences with anxiety was most helpful in dealing with my disorder. When I was struggling with anxiety I initially turned to internet research and books written by professionals for information and advice. While these resources did help, I found that often times the discussion from the professional's point of view made me feel simply like another statistic with a medical problem. I never found any comfort in learning that I was an incremental part of the more than forty million people in this world who suffer from an anxiety disorder and/or depression (*www.adaa.org* and *www.HealthLine.com*). It wasn't until I spoke with my good friends and family about my struggle with anxiety that I began to find comfort. Just about each one of them had experienced abnormal anxiety at some point in their lives, some even to the point of developing a disorder. They were all average everyday people, much like me, who dealt with thoughts and feelings similar to the way I did. I began to realize that "abnormal" anxiety was, in fact, quite common. This was extremely surprising for me to learn!

Most people don't openly discuss their struggles with anxiety or depression because our society has attached such a negative stigma to these conditions. Anxiety and depression are often thought of as affecting only weak-minded or unsuccessful people and so it is this stigma that prevents many people from openly sharing their battles with others. In fact, all of the close people in my life that I spoke to only shared their stories with me because I broached the subject and shared my personal struggles with them first. Thankfully I did, because it was these stories that gave me a sense of normalcy and acceptance, and a great deal of hope. I no longer felt like a statistic.

There were so many people around me who had been through similar struggles with anxiety (or were experiencing them at that time) and had prospered and grown from those challenges. This newfound realization lifted me from my state of despair and uncertainty. This knowledge empowered me, restoring the confidence I so desperately needed to help me free myself from the hold that my anxiety disorder had on my life. I am hoping that my story will do the same for you.

This book will introduce you to anxiety, its symptoms, and its causes. It will also outline fifteen key strategies for dealing with anxiety that I developed as a result of my experiences. In fact, my stories and strategies became valuable information for many friends and peers who I spoke with after my anxiety ordeal. It helped many of them who were suffering from anxiety, and those who were developing certain *thinking traps* that would have surely led them into a battle with anxiety. In fact, I finally decided to write this book after sharing my *Cheat Sheet* (Chapter 10) with a good friend who called me the next day to let me know how much my experiences and advice had helped her. It was at that moment that I realized I had something valuable that I needed to share with others.

1

The Attack

January twenty-fifth is a day I won't soon forget. It began the same as any other day—with a newspaper and a cup of coffee. I sat at my desk reading an article about six alleged terrorists suspected to be on the run in Boston and had been surprised about the story. Why Boston? Were these terrorists lost or confused? I brushed it off, not taking the story too seriously. In fact, I remember being more concerned about yesterday's five-cent fall in my company's stock price than a potential terrorist threat.

The morning progressed, and I was soon sitting in a conference room on the thirty-sixth floor of the Prudential Center in Boston, readying myself for a meeting. It was my first month in a new position and I wanted to make sure that I was on top of things and learning as much as I possibly could. I sat next to a few colleagues, listening to the head of our company speak.

Suddenly, the lights flickered and the talking ceased. The room then went dark for a moment. As the lights regained their illumination, someone in the room joked that it might be the terrorists trying to blow up the building. Most people chuckled, and then continued discussing the topic at hand.

Unfortunately, it wasn't that simple for me. A sudden rush of adrenaline shot through my body and into my head. It hit me out of the blue and felt as though someone had sucked the breath out of my lungs and blew it back into my face. I was almost knocked out of my chair. It made me feel instantly dizzy to the point where I thought I might pass out. My heart had started pounding stronger and faster making me feel like I was having a heart attack! I had absolutely no idea what was going on. I had never had feelings like this before. All of these sensations, from the heart palpitations to the rush of adrenaline, were new to me.

Then, as quickly as the episode came on, it seemed to stop. The adrenaline rush subsided, yet

I still felt very dizzy and off balance, similar to how you would feel if you stood up too quickly after sitting down for an extended period of time. I was hot and sweaty. It was only after the feelings had passed that I realized that my body had sweated profusely. My shirt was drenched and stuck to me in an incredibly uncomfortable way. The sweat soon turned cold, like ice water all over my body, and I began shivering. A strange, innate sensation to get out of that confined room came over me. I had never felt that way before but knew I needed to leave—immediately. My colleagues were oblivious to what had just happened to me so I grabbed my things and quietly left the room.

I was perplexed. What in the world could have caused such a strange reaction? I sat down at my desk, still feeling dizzy, trying to regain my composure. Ten minutes later I felt better physically but still uncertain both mentally and emotionally. Could it have been the air circulation in the conference room? Maybe it was less efficient than what I was used to? I rationalized this answer in my mind, deciding that the poor circulation was to blame for my bizarre reactions.

As coincidence would have it, I had dinner that night with my father who was in town on business. As we caught up on my new position, responsibilities, and my recent move from New York City to Boston, I also mentioned the strange "attack" from earlier that day. He too was confused and, like any concerned parent, told me to watch it and let him and a doctor know if it happened again. He also classified it as a one time thing, agreeing with my conclusion that it was most likely caused by the poor circulation in the conference room. I felt relieved, and from there our discussion turned to my beloved Red Sox and our excitement about their upcoming season! I was no longer concerned about the strange attack, and in fact, it would not cross my mind again until nine days later.

2

Developing an Anxiety Disorder

The following week I was on a business trip in Seattle. My colleague and I were in a small conference room giving a presentation to one of our customers. Once I had finished my portion of the presentation, I sat down to listen to my colleague finish up. Suddenly, I felt a quick, strong surge of adrenaline rush to my head. I was short of breath, my heart began pounding irregularly, and I started to feel as though I was going to pass out. I thought about how embarrassing it would be if that happened in front of my colleague and my new clients. Again, I felt a powerful desire to get out of that room. But it was impossible to leave at that moment. Somehow, I pulled myself together and finished the meeting without notice from my colleague or my clients. However, unbeknownst to me at the time, this attack changed my life forever. No longer was my first attack a "one-time thing". I knew then that it had not been caused by the poor circulation in a particular conference room back in

Boston. I knew then that there was something wrong with *me*.

Traveling home the following day, I had an eerie feeling about getting on the plane and being confined for four to five hours. This was new to me. I had never minded flying before, nor had I ever been bothered by confined settings, be it a conference room, a plane, or even a car. But I kept thinking about what had happened the day before. I even replayed both attacks over in my mind repeatedly. I wondered what was going on with me and worried that it might be something physical. Then my fears started to spiral out of control. Rather attempt to understand what and why these two attacks had happened, I began thinking about the future, worrying that I wouldn't be able to do my job effectively, or even at all, if the attacks persisted. I started to fear passing out in future meetings, in front of colleagues, clients, or worse, perhaps my new boss. I pictured what might happen if I passed out in a meeting. What would I say? These thoughts continued the entire plane ride home and as I lay in bed awake that night. I didn't sleep much.

The next day we had a company meeting in a large hotel ballroom attached to our office building. I tentatively entered the huge room, feeling anxious and scared immediately. It was as though my mind was fighting my body not to go in. I was afraid of having another attack in front of my entire company, and potentially passing out. I pushed through the nervous feelings and took a seat. I lasted for about ten minutes, before *another* attack hit. I quickly got up, left the room, and raced to the bathroom where I splashed water on my face. How could this be happening again?! Ten minutes later, I thought about returning to the meeting but couldn't. It was the first time in my life that I didn't do something because I was afraid, and it was the first time in my life that I felt truly defeated.

I had no idea what was happening to me. I was confused and scared because I couldn't control the attacks. My first three attacks had all included similar symptoms—sweating, dizziness, adrenaline rushes throughout my body, and severe heart palpitations. Many times my heart pounded so hard on my chest that I thought I was having a heart attack. For these reasons, I was convinced there was something wrong with me physically. I went back to my desk shaking and almost in tears. I didn't know what to do. I called my general practitioner and scheduled an immediate appointment for the following day. I packed up my computer and walked home.

I can remember that strange walk home vividly. My mind was filled with a million thoughts and feelings. I was confused, scared, sad, and mad all at the same time. I felt hopeless, inferior, and most of all, trapped. I knew I was dealing with something that I couldn't simply walk away from, or leave behind. I knew that once I got home I'd still have a serious problem to deal with, and that when the next day arrived and I went to work, I'd *still* have the problem. I never thought I'd feel this way at age twenty-nine, especially after having lived such a fortunate life with very few problems or complications. I felt weak and ashamed.

After walking for a while, I came across a homeless man sitting on the street corner, cold, dirty, and hunched over. A strong desire to trade places with this man quickly entered my mind, and I was shocked—that was certainly the mindset of a desperate person. As this homeless man was hunched over, he looked up at me and said, "I am a loser and I have nothing. Can you spare any change?"

I was so deep in thought that what he said, or even the fact that he had spoken, didn't register with me until I had taken another five steps. Once it hit me, I froze in my tracks. It suddenly occurred to me how sad, hopeless, and lost this man was and how much he lacked any sense of well-being or self-worth. And strangely enough, at that moment I felt as if I could relate to him. The frightening part was that I actually wanted to trade lives with him right there on that sidewalk just to escape my troubles. With the state of mind I was in at that time, I would have thought about trading places with anyone.

But this homeless man hit home. His state at the time and what he said to me hit home. I turned and walked back toward him. He grimaced with what I assume was fear, wondering what I was going to do or say. I looked him in the eye and, before I had the chance to formulate what I was going to say, I started speaking, "Listen, you are not a loser. Why would you say that? Don't think that way about yourself."

The man stared at me, completely and utterly confused. I'm sure he was shocked that I cared about what he thought of himself or what he had said about himself, or even that I had stopped to talk to him. And I was just as confused. Why had I felt compelled to say something to this man? Maybe it was because I felt dejected and inadequate at that moment and it irked me to know that somebody else might be feeling that same way? I knew I couldn't offer this man much help, nor could my few words solve his problems, so I did the only thing I could at the time to help— I gave him money and made him promise that he would no longer call himself, or think of himself, as a loser.

When I finally arrived home it was still early, about two o'clock in the afternoon. I had only walked two miles from my office, yet it seemed like I had been walking all day. I have a foggy memory of the few hours that followed. I turned on the television but was not able to digest a word I heard. I tried to take a nap but of course wasn't able to fall asleep. The one thing I was able to do throughout that afternoon was worry about the next day at work.

I called my older sister later that night. She and I are close in age and have always had a great relationship. We've been able to talk about everything, even those things I never spoke about to my parents or to my other sister. I called her and asked how she was doing. Immediately she knew something was wrong. I told her what had happened that day, and about my other attacks. Like me, she was confused and didn't have much advice to offer. But she was a great listener and even offered to drive up from Connecticut and spend the night with me. I thanked her but had known even then that that wouldn't be the answer to my problems. I needed to get through this on my own, but it did feel great to have someone to talk to. I desperately needed that.

During the days and weeks that followed, I constantly thought about my problem, searching for some sort of answer or resolution. Unfortunately, no solutions came to mind, and unknowingly, I was making matters much worse by constantly thinking and worrying about the issue. I also spent a great deal of time in and out of my doctor's office, undergoing tests for my heart, asthma, and stress. I even wore a heart monitor for forty-eight hours to determine whether or not I had an irregular heartbeat or weak heart activity. Yet, through all of it, I went to work each day with a smile on my face and I didn't show one sign of a problem. However, behind that fake smile and happy façade, I was more scared than ever. I wasn't sleeping and had lost my appetite. I was upset and angry and consumed by the physical effects that I continued to experience. I went to work everyday dizzy, tentative, and unsure of what would happen at any given moment. I shied away from meetings and public conversations. I felt claustrophobic in enclosed conference rooms, and found myself pacing back and forth quite often. The only time I felt alright was when I was in motion, when I was walking, running, or simply out in an open area and moving.

A few weeks later, my test results came in. My general practitioner, a good friend of mine, called me to tell me that he had both good and bad news. I tensed up. He continued, "The good news is that your heart is very strong and healthy and physically you are fine. In fact, you are in great shape and healthier than most young men your age. The bad news is that . . .," he paused, "you're crazy."

Of course he was kidding; however he did know that the issues and attacks I had been experiencing were not caused by physical ailments, but rather by anxiety. He suggested that I contact our company Employee Assistance Program (EAP) and discuss the situation with someone there.

But I disagreed. I didn't feel that I needed to talk to anybody. Just as I had done for my entire life, I would handle this issue on my own. Help? I didn't need help. I was a successful, confident, strong man—right? In my mind, all I needed to do was take a step back, fix what was wrong, and I'd be fine. Plus, I was skeptical about talking to someone about my problems. I assumed psychological therapy was for people who were incapable of handling their own problems.

3

Introduction to Anxiety

Anxiety, fear, panic, and depression—they can affect any of us at any time. In fact, when I first developed my anxiety disorder I was on top of the world. My career was thriving and I had been recently promoted. Not long before that I had finished graduate school and received my MBA. I'd also purchased my first home. I was healthy, happy, very active, and had a great family and a close group of friends. I felt extremely fortunate and this should have been reflected in my feelings. Yet something was off. Rather than enjoying my life and all of the things that I had accomplished, I found myself stressed and anxious about my future. I was torn between where I was and where I thought I should be.

As my anxiety grew, I began to educate myself about anxiety disorders, panic attacks, and depression. What I learned was that successful, intelligent, hard-working, highly-motivated people (much like myself) are more likely to be affected by anxiety than others. Our drive for perfection (I am a pseudo-perfectionist) leaves us susceptible to anxiety. Additionally, our intelligence gives us the ability to understand anxiety while also playing out its potentially disastrous effects in our minds. This intelligence and drive for perfection leads to over-thinking which then only generates more anxiety.

What's interesting is that anxiety itself, when understood and kept in check, can be a positive attribute and characteristic. It's what drives us to achieve, be successful, move forward and grow in life. However, similar to the way I grew up, most people don't realize that we actually need to manage our anxiety in order to prevent it from spiraling out of control and develop into a disorder. Anxiety can become so strong and all-encompassing that it can drive people into depression. Over 80% of the time, anxiety and depression coexist (*www.HealthLine.com*).

Anxiety is growing exponentially in our society. Anxiety disorders (including depression) now currently affect well over 10% of Americans each year, that's roughly forty million people (*www.adaa.org* and *www.HealthLine.com*). This percentage has increased significantly from earlier decades and many professionals attribute this rise to the differences in today's world compared to those of worlds past. Today's young Americans have many more choices and opportunities available to them compared to older generations. Many people now get married and start families later in life and spend a great deal more time focusing on themselves and their careers. In 2005, single unmarried households surpassed married households as the most common household dynamic (over 22%) in the United States and researchers believe this trend will continue (*Northwestern National Life*).

In addition to a substantial increase in opportunities, many careers have become much more demanding and intense with the advances in the technology and communication sector. Can you imagine trying to get your job done *without* email, cell phones, or your trusty Blackberry? Or better yet, can you imagine trying to get away from your job *with* these things? The increased stressors in life, along with the more abundant opportunities, have significantly changed our society compared to when our grandparents and parents grew up. Today, 25% of US employees view their jobs and their careers as the # 1 stressor in their lives (*Northwestern National Life*). Also, 75% of the American workforce believe today's worker has more on the job stress than a generation ago (*Princeton Survey Research Association*). Times have changed.

When I first spoke to my parents regarding my struggle with anxiety, they did not know what advice to offer. Like me, they spent weeks reading books and online information regarding General Anxiety Disorders (GAD), Panic Disorders, Social Anxiety Disorder (SAD), Obsessive Compulsive Disorder (OCD), Attention Deficit Disorder (ADD), Post Traumatic Disorder, and Clinical Depression. As we educated ourselves, we learned how prevalent anxiety disorders are in today's society. I can remember speaking to my father who put it best when he said, "Son, my life was much easier. I went to high school and made it to college. I felt fortunate for that opportunity. I graduated, got married, got a job to support us, and very soon started our family. Life was much simpler; I didn't have the choices or the opportunities that you have. I worked to support your mother and three children, bought a house, and the years rolled by. I never stopped to think any differently. Today, I look at your life and the lives of your peers—you all graduate from college, live in big cities, travel, focus more on yourselves, and take your time finding a mate. With more opportunities and decisions I would assume comes more anxiety."

My father was correct. His perspective supported the fact that the number of *reported* anxiety disorders has almost doubled in the last two decades. Because anxiety disorders are growing at such a large clip across the country, it's no secret that the society in which we live is a major reason for this. Just open the morning paper—today's media culture constantly bombards us with sensationalism regarding terrorism, war, global warming, murders, health issues, and many other stressful topics. Each new day brings more bad news adding yet another layer of anxiety to our lives.

But it's not these issues that worry me; I realize that they are out of our control. My major concern is that education about anxiety is not growing as rapidly. Without education or knowledge, you would not be able to identify symptoms and signs of an anxiety disorder. Nor would you be able to understand how to manage anxiety if and when it strikes. Also, you might have little understanding about how your personality can lead you down a road toward an anxiety disorder. Minimal knowledge about the symptoms and effects of anxiety will make its impact on you much more severe. Educating yourself about anxiety before it strikes will lessen the blow, if not protect you from it altogether.

Let me explain—imagine being a professional baseball player, up to bat against Randy Johnson, an amazing pitcher, in the bottom of the ninth inning. Your team is down by two runs and the bases are loaded. The count is full, three and two. Now ask yourself, would you want to know what pitch he is going to throw? Fastball or curveball? Eighty or ninety-five miles per hour? Would you want to know what to expect, perhaps even where he will throw it, inside or outside? Low or at your head? Wouldn't your chances of hitting that ball be much greater if you knew what was coming, rather than being caught off guard with the pitch? Granted, you may or may not hit this ball, but your chances of dealing with this opportunity are much greater the more knowledge you have about the imminent pitch. It is similar with anxiety. If you understand the effects anxiety can have on your mind, body, and well-being, you'll be much better equipped to manage it, fight it, and potentially avoid developing a disorder, regardless of how well you can swing a baseball bat!

In addition to society's lack of knowledge about anxiety there also exists a negative stereotype associated with cognitive behavioral therapy, otherwise known as "talk therapy". My initial reaction to my own anxiety problem—that I could handle it on my own—is often times the attitude of many people in our society. This type of thinking makes most people shy away from admitting that they need counseling—I know because it's what made me shy away from it. The first step in conquering an anxiety disorder is admitting to yourself that you need help and that it's okay to seek it. It's also important to realize that having an anxiety disorder does not mean that you are weak, ignorant, unsuccessful, or inferior. As I described at the start of this chapter, it means just the opposite—motivated, successful, intelligent people suffer from anxiety issues because they care so much about their lives, their future, and are constantly striving for the best. They push themselves to succeed and can only live with doing just that. I wish I had made the decision to speak with someone sooner during my struggle with anxiety, for it would have taught me how to deal with my extremely anxious feelings and might have even prevented my anxiety from festering and developing into a disorder altogether.

Our generation's ignorance is exemplified in my own story. Before the onset of my anxiety disorder, I never even knew anxiety could reach the level of a disorder. I never assumed anxiety could become detrimental to my mental and physical health. If I had I would never have let it develop the way it did. I wouldn't have had to spend months educating myself while fearing each ensuing day. Although, then I wouldn't be here today telling you my story. I wouldn't have had the opportunity to turn this unfortunate and dreadful experience into a positive one. For months I lost control of my life, my self-esteem, my happiness and my well-being. I lost hope, along with the love of life I once possessed. Professionals say anxiety disorders can lead to depression. Now I can see why. Anxiety can take the enjoyment out of life if you let it and if left untreated, depression is sure to follow.

But there is hope and I am living proof of that. Anxiety surely knocked me down, but it couldn't keep me down. I stood back up, and I'm not only enjoying life today the way I once did, I am enjoying it in a much more fulfilling way. I can remember endlessly hoping to one day feel the way I used to. Well, that never did happen—I actually feel better than ever.

4

Who Am I?

So what type of person gets burdened by an anxiety disorder? If you knew me, would you think I was susceptible to such a condition? My friends surely didn't. My family didn't either. In fact, anyone whom I shared my struggles with was surprised. Most viewed me as a young man who had it all. And from the outside, I was. I had my health, a very loving family, and a great group of friends. I grew up very blessed. I was lucky to be an athletic kid and a high school three-sport All-State athlete. My fortune continued in college where I received a baseball scholarship, became a Division I NCAA All-American, and captained that baseball team. I also made the Dean's List at this nationally acclaimed university and graduated with Cum Laude Honors. My good fortune and luck didn't stop there. I went to work for a Fortune 500 company immediately after graduating from college. I had a great job and enjoyed a promising career. Financially, I was very comfortable and stable and I owned my own home. What more could I have asked for? I had everything I had wanted. Oh, and something I didn't want—a very serious anxiety disorder.

I tell you these things about me not to boast but to illustrate the fact that anxiety disorders can affect even the most fortunate of people. I was always under the impression that my experiences, particularly those involving athletics, would equip me with the ability to succeed under pressure and provide me with sound coping skills. I never thought I'd get knocked down by an anxiety disorder. In fact, people who know me were shocked to hear that I was struggling with anxiety. One of my very best friends was no different when I first told him about my problem. "You? You have anxiety? Wow, I always looked at you as someone who had the world in his hands, who was always happy and jovial. I never would have associated you with anxiety, never mind an anxiety disorder." I chuckled and told him that prior to its onset, I wouldn't have associated myself with an anxiety disorder either.

When I was faced with the reality that I had developed an anxiety disorder, I felt ashamed, weak, and secluded. I hadn't even heard much about the disorder. I thought an anxious person was someone who had too much energy. I thought depression was for sad and moody people. I never knew such disorders could affect me (or anyone I knew), especially at the point in my life when anxiety hit me. What I didn't realize was that I had let stress build up inside of me and eventually turn into anxiety. I stumbled upon a quarter-life crisis due to a combination of this stress and the fact that I was constantly focusing on my future. I was dwelling on where I thought I should be rather than simply being happy with where I was.

Thinking about the future and not living for the present day is the number one cause of anxiety. Anxiety is an emotion directly linked with thoughts based on future events, situations, or worries. By focusing on the present, you can significantly reduce your chances of dealing with severe anxiety. Think about it: by focusing on the present moment you aren't worrying about the future, and therefore your stress and anxiety levels decrease.

I didn't know this at the time. I allowed the thoughts of my future and what I thought I *should* be doing at my age to cloud my enjoyment of the present. I didn't realize that the thoughts I was having were detrimental to my health and my well-being. As I pondered the *what ifs* and *shoulds* in my future my anxiety began to grow out of control, heading for a disorder. Because I knew nothing about anxiety disorders, I stayed the course and never foresaw what lay ahead.

5

A Child—A Future Thinker

It's quite amazing that I didn't truly know myself until my struggle with anxiety. Prior to that, if you had asked me if I was an anxious person I would have said no. It wasn't until I had developed an anxiety disorder and learned more about myself that I realized how wrong I was. I have always been an anxious person.

When I look back at my childhood I now see an anxious child who strived to succeed in everything that he did. I never settled for less, I always had to win, and I usually had to be in control. I was a perfectionist, although never admitted or even realized this fact. Perhaps it stemmed from being the youngest of three children. Many people have said that the youngest child always pushes the hardest to prove him or herself. In addition, I had to contend with my two older sisters who were great students and even better athletes. In fact, they were exceptional athletes. They both received full athletic scholarships to college, and were recognized nationally as two of the best female athletes of their respective eras. I guess you can say they left large footprints for me to fill. And fill them I set out to do.

I am sure that this dynamic between my sisters and I had a lot to do with the personality that I developed to always succeed. Filling those footprints, and trying to make them even bigger with my own imprint, was my motivation. But I never looked at this determination as a negative. In fact, I always viewed it as a positive. This attitude didn't allow me to settle for C's or D's in school. It pushed me to make sure that I received A's and B's. My determination didn't allow me to be just a participant in a group; I had to be the leader. And it certainly didn't allow me to settle for being a mediocre athlete; I had to be the best.

So, have I always an anxious person? As I spent time looking back at my life I began to realize that, yes, I have. When I was younger, I was always thinking ahead. Thinking of what I could do or achieve next rather than enjoying the present moment. If I was doing a project, I was rushing to get it done to begin what came next. If I was walking down the hall, I was rushing to get to my destination. It even showed in the way I ate. If I needed to leave, I could devour two sandwiches and a tall glass of milk in two minutes and be out the door and on my way. It seemed like I always had something to do or somewhere to go. That was my life as I grew up. In fact, I can still hear my father today. He was always telling me to *slow down*. He and I didn't do many projects around the house together because I would rush to get it done as he would take his time and make sure we were doing it right. Ten minutes into it, he'd be telling me to slow down while I'd be annoyed that he was taking so long.

As I grew up, graduated high school, and went to college, my way of living continued. I played baseball in college, worked hard in the classroom, and managed to have a very active social life. These parts of my life didn't leave much time for anything else. I remember shuffling from class to class, to practice, to the dining hall, and then rushing home after the day was over to hang out with my friends. I didn't even sleep much because I never wanted to miss anything. My life was filled with always doing one thing after another. At that time I felt as though my life was extremely enjoyable.

Once I graduated from college, I immediately went to work. I accepted a highly sought after position in my present company's training program and began what has transpired into a great career. In the nine years that I have been with this company I have held eight different positions, most of them with increased responsibility. Looking back I see that I was constantly looking ahead to my next job. I always knew what I needed to do in order to be successful in each of the positions I held and I worked hard to do just that with the sole intention of being promoted. Looking back, I wish I had learned earlier to enjoy where I was at each stage of my career rather than having spent so much time worrying about where I was going to go next. I missed some of the enjoyment of each job and the satisfaction of settling into each position. In the road of life, especially in terms of your career, it's important to enjoy some down time every now and then and be happy with your accomplishments and where you are. You can very easily burn out if you don't.

I can pinpoint many other circumstances throughout my life where I was looking ahead and passing up the enjoyment of the present moment. Two years ago, I had shoulder surgery. I waited for the summer to end and my job to slow down before having the surgery. I was planning on spending the week after surgery at my parent's summer home on the shore of Massachusetts. Obviously surgery is not fun, but I did look forward to a week off from work, a week-long stay at my folk's summer home, and most importantly, a week of pampering from my retired mother who planned on nursing me back to health. A little rest and relaxation was on the horizon.

The surgery went well and I was home and resting by mid-afternoon. I didn't experience much pain and my recovery would be rather fast and easy. Each morning, I would grab a coffee and take a long walk along the beach. I would end up down by the marina and watch the boats come in and out for a few hours while I sat and read the paper. I remember each day being perfect October weather—roughly sixty-five degrees and sunny. Basically, I couldn't have asked for anything more. But rather than enjoy this week to my full potential, I spent most of it worrying about what my next job would be, when it would happen, and what I truly wanted to do with my life. I let a valuable week pass me by.

Looking back at this week after learning so much about anxiety and the importance of enjoying the present moment, I realize I didn't enjoy those days the way that I could have. I was stressed and uneasy the entire week. During my daily walks, I would obsess over my next promotion. When would it come? What would it be? Would I be happy with it? Would it be in Boston like I had planned? What if it wasn't the job I wanted? Or at the level I wanted? All of these thoughts and worries occupied my mind. They took the place of the enjoyment I could have had during those days. The weather was beautiful, I was on a beach, I had no work and my parents were cooking me great meals each day. Unfortunately, all I remember was wishing I had my next job and career move figured out so that I could relax and stop worrying.

To this day it bothers me that I didn't enjoy myself that week but more so because I wasted time and energy constantly worrying about things that were out of my control. I was worried about what was going to come my way professionally and personally without knowing what opportunities lay ahead or what fate had in store for me. It's impossible to predict what jobs might open up or what opportunities might present themselves down the road. It's all a matter of chance and worrying about them is truly a huge waste of time, energy, and opportunity.

I now realize that I let a great week slip by, but this realization is better late than never. I now understand how and where I strayed at that time, and I won't make that mistake again. As you will see, my experiences in regard to my battle with anxiety have given me the ability to focus much more of my energy on the enjoyment of the present moment. I no longer revert back to my old habit of exerting my thoughts on distant and future events and worrying about what's to come—especially things out of my control and left to chance. It's now clear to me that it's important to plan for the future, but much more important to live in, and for, the moment.

6

What Is Going On With Me?

There sure is something humbling about developing an anxiety disorder. No matter your age or how fortunate of a life you have lived, an anxiety disorder can knock you down in a heartbeat. At the onset of my disorder, I felt as though I was losing my identity. The thoughts and fears I began to have weren't typical for me. And as time went on, I allowed those fears to turn me into a different person. The disorder seemed to negate the majority of my life's previous experiences and accomplishments which had defined who I was. The memories of my life before anxiety were virtually nonexistent—no longer did I think about my happy childhood, the great experiences I had in college, meeting friends, playing baseball, or enjoying my career. My panic attacks caused me to lose control of my emotions and my thoughts, and I focused solely on the anxiety issues that plagued my life. It became increasingly difficult for me to get through even the most mundane daily activities, both in my professional life, and eventually, my personal life.

I began to fear that I was this new anxiety-filled person. That all of the feelings and thoughts that were plaguing me were the *new me*, and the worst part about this—I didn't like the new me. I didn't like being afraid when going to work, heading to dinner with friends, standing in line, or even attending church. And I especially didn't like feeling uncomfortable sitting on my couch in my own home! The most frustrating part was that I felt this way at a point in my life when I had considered myself to be a strong, experienced, secure man. The *old me* never thought twice about doing any of these things, yet after my anxiety set in, doing them became such a challenge that I no longer enjoyed them. I didn't stop to think that if these experiences had not bothered me for twenty-eight years, I'd find a way to enjoy them once again. I really saw no light at the end of this tunnel.

Because my first few panic attacks occurred during meetings while I was at work, this largely impacted my comfort level during meetings and other professional situations. That is where I began to have my initial challenges with severe anxiety. Each day, I hoped to get through work and any scheduled meeting without another attack. The moment I knew I would have another meeting an inner uneasiness would ring throughout my mind and body. I began to feel defeated, ashamed, and weak. All I'd want to do was escape my professional working environment. How was I going to get through this?

And so it was then that I made a promise to myself—I would never let my fears or feelings dictate my actions. I would never skip or cancel a meeting. My fears and thoughts may have owned the way I felt inside but I promised myself that they wouldn't control my actions or stop me from doing my job. I attended one meeting after another with a renewed sense of determination. Of course each instance produced anything but normal feelings. I'd begin to sweat profusely, my heart would palpitate uncontrollably, I'd be dizzy and feel clammy and I'd constantly fight my inner reaction to flee (which my body produced from the moment I would enter the meeting). I used every piece of courage and energy I had to muscle through each and every single meeting.

My life as I knew it had changed. Every hour, minute, and even second, was a battle against anxiety. Two months after my first attack, a typical day for me included waking up by five in the morning and tossing and turning for two hours. Many times I'd lie there and stare at the ceiling. Other times, I'd drift in and out of sleep for twenty minutes here or there. Prior to my anxiety disorder I'd sleep straight through the night and early morning, usually until my alarm clock went off at seven o'clock. But with anxiety, I found myself constantly awake, thinking about how much time was left before I'd need to get out of bed, and I hated that feeling. The thought of getting up, showering, and heading into work, where I'd spend the day anxious and fearful, did not appeal to me. But with the combination of courage and the promise I had made to myself to never let anxiety control me I got up each morning and started my day—anxious, depressed, and uneasy.

Walking into my office building, I'd worry about what that day had in store for me. Would I have another attack? Would anyone notice? Would I be able to do my job? Would this day be a good or bad day? All of these thoughts plagued my mind and, many times, the remnants from the previous days' experiences would bring vivid flashbacks that would make me cringe. I'd then anticipate similar experiences for the coming day and by doing so I'd provoke my own anxiety. Simple things like getting into a crowded elevator or standing in line to get my morning coffee frustrated me and I began to dread them.

In my office I'd feel off-balance, dizzy, and preoccupied. Getting my mind involved in a project or on my work was a struggle. I constantly focused on my disorder and the way I was feeling rather than thinking about my job. I was sincerely struggling to find the life that I once knew and the person I once was. I felt my job and my career were suffering and I'd produce more anxiety by worrying about whether or not these horrible feelings would persist. My day would pass painfully and I wouldn't even have a desire to eat (although I'd force myself to in order to stay healthy). In the evening, I'd go to the gym before heading home. It was usually tough to muster up the motivation to work out, but I was adamant to keep myself in shape. I had read that exercise is one of the most important activities for battling anxiety and/or depression and I was determined to stick with it. But, most times I felt so drained and tired that I had to really push myself to run even short distances. Plus, breathing was quite difficult because my anxiety kept my chest and lungs constricted.

After the gym, I'd finally return home. Rather than enjoy my down time and leisure activities, I found myself already thinking about going through the same stressful routine the next day. I'd spend countless hours worrying about the way I thought I would feel. I had trouble enjoying my leisure time knowing that I would soon have to return to the office. My typical day would end around midnight and I'd lie in bed staring at my ceiling, struggling to fall asleep. Most nights my mind continuously raced with worries. During the height of my anxiety disorder, I probably only averaged about three hours of sleep a night.

Three months after the arrival of my disorder, I went home to visit my parents for a weekend. Traditional Sunday mornings involved a family outing to church. Yet this time, my visit to church was different. As I sat there I felt what, at that time, had become familiar and frightening feelings—sweating, dizziness, and the urge to flee. But I wasn't at work nor was I nervous or anxious about anything in particular that morning, how could these reactions be happening? What I didn't realize was that I *was* nervous and anxious. I was nervous about the anxiety and the attacks that I had been dealing with over the past few months. I was nervous about having another attack. Just because I was away from work and not in a meeting didn't mean my mind was free from the fears and thoughts that accompanied my anxiety disorder. That was the first time I suffered an anxiety attack in a place not related to work; and it wouldn't be the last.

About two weeks after that, I went to breakfast on a Saturday morning with a bunch of friends. Again I found myself uncomfortable, fidgety, and preoccupied during the entire meal. I even had minor heart palpitations and sweat through my shirt. I noticed that my legs constantly twitched and bounced up and down under the table, always in motion. I also kept glancing at the door in case I needed to leave. And I knew then that it had happened—I had allowed anxiety to infiltrate every part of my life.

Although my anxiety had stemmed from my professional pressures, it was no longer segregated to that area of my life. I began to experience displeasure from social events and experiences that I had once enjoyed tremendously. I became so worried about having additional attacks that I actually feared the attacks themselves. No longer was I focused on the stress or pressure that had brought on my attacks. The attacks had taken on lives of their own. My mind had shown my body a way to physically react to my feelings and my body had begun to follow that path routinely. With the hint of any anxious thoughts or feelings, my body immediately tensed up and generated more anxiety. This was a dangerous and extremely difficult cycle to break.

In early April I had two tickets to the Boston Red Sox opening day game versus the New York Yankees. I invited my best friend and we skipped out of work early to catch the pre-game ceremony and festivities. It was chilly that day but sunny and bright and it felt great to be out of work. Yet to my surprise, as soon as we sat down I began to feel uncomfortable. My mind fixated on all of the horrible experiences that I had been dealing with. What would I do if I had an attack then? Would people notice? How could I get out of the stadium? As I continued down that path of thinking I grew increasingly uncomfortable and I began sweating profusely, I felt dizzy, and my heart started to pound faster and faster. This continued on and off until about the fifth inning when I started to feel more comfortable. It seemed as if I had finally adapted to my surroundings and had begun to relax. I was slowly able to focus my energy and thoughts on other things including the game, my surroundings, and the present moment rather than worry about having another attack. I got through the baseball game, and even enjoyed some of it!

Although I had a glimpse of hope at the baseball game, the following week I was not as fortunate. I had a dentist appointment a few days later and as I anxiously sat in the waiting room, I anticipated a challenge in being confined to a chair for thirty minutes. I fixated on the way I thought I would feel during the experience and by the time the nurse called me in, I had already replayed the uncomfortable situation in my head a few times. My anxiety was on alert and I anticipated the worst. As the dentist cleaned my teeth my mind raced feverishly. I began sweating profusely and my heart pounded tremendously. This feeling lasted for about fifteen minutes and then passed. I left the appointment feeling very defeated, depressed, and angry, yet again.

Not too long after that appointment, I was scheduled to go on a vacation with a group of close friends. We had planned a trip to the Bahamas and for the first time in my life I felt very uncomfortable at the thought of traveling, almost to the point where I wanted to cancel the vacation. It was to be a week full of relaxation, partying, and quality time with my good friends. Perhaps this was just what I needed to take my mind off of the anxiety that was plaguing me. Very quickly I realized this would not be the case—it would soon turn into another wasted week of worrying just like the week I spent recovering from shoulder surgery.

While on vacation I'd rethink every anxious moment and episode that I had had in the three months prior and I'd worry about dealing with those same experiences when I returned. Rather than providing me with rest and relaxation I so desperately needed, it soon became obvious that the trip would only compound my anxiety problem. I was preoccupied with my own thoughts day after day. And because I couldn't shake things, for the first time I began to feel depressed. Most nights I didn't even want to go out, I'd rather lie in bed and watch television. I felt safer and more comfortable in my dark hotel room where I could drift in and out of sleep. When I slept, it was the only time my mind was free of constant worry and anxiety. Though of course, I could never sleep well. When it comes to sleep, having anxiety is like having children. The more children you have, the more sleep you need, but the less you actually get.

On my way home from the Bahamas my flight had a layover in Miami and I had three hours to kill in the airport. I was distraught after my failure to enjoy myself on vacation and I dreaded the thought of heading back to my life in Boston. I felt that if I couldn't even enjoy a vacation then all was hopeless. That day, I think for a few hours in the Miami International Airport, I gave up. I couldn't even sit down and wait for my flight. I paced back and forth between terminals not knowing what to do. I seriously contemplated renting a car and driving all the way back to Boston but knew that that wouldn't solve my problem. I thankfully still had enough common sense to realize that I'd hate myself for such a decision five hours into the twenty hour drive. I continued to pace back and forth frantically. Finally, I found a corner of the American Airlines terminal, called my mother, and cried for an hour on the phone. I completely broke down. I told her I didn't know what to do or what was going on with me. I told her I felt hopeless and helpless and that I wanted to just give up. I had hit rock bottom. I wanted to quit my job and move back home to the town in which I grew up, where my parents were still living. I got so wrapped up in my own despair that I thought that was the answer to my problems. My mind was looking for a comfortable solution and leaving the job and life that I created in Boston for my childhood home in Connecticut felt like my only option.

7

Steps in Therapy

A few hours later, after I had calmed down, I realized that quitting my job and moving home weren't the right choices nor would they solve my problems. It was clear that I could not run from my anxiety for it would follow me anywhere. My life was in Boston and my battle with anxiety needed to be there as well. Plus, I don't just give up.

After much hesitation and procrastination I took the advice of my general practitioner and contacted my company's employee assistance program representative shortly after I arrived home from my "vacation" to the Bahamas. I did not know what to expect from my first meeting with the representative, Catherine Baker. I sat down and began to tell her what was troubling me. She was a very good listener and paid close attention to what I said. I began describing my new job, my move back to Boston, my uncertainty about what I wanted to do with my life, the pressure I put on myself to grow up, and the anxiety and panic attacks that I had experienced. We spoke for an hour. She was a wonderful listener and offered great insight into my situation.

Over the next few weeks I continued to meet with Catherine. She suggested I get in touch with *The Mind/Body Medical Institute* (Brookline, Massachusetts; www.mbmi.org) to speak with a psychiatrist there because her contract with my company allowed her only a fixed number of sessions with each employee. Therefore, her approach to working with me differed from a therapist who didn't have such limitations. Because of my inexperience with therapy, I subconsciously hoped that our limited time together would suffice. I felt that getting to know one therapist was enough for me at that point. So I continued to see Catherine and we discussed everything that had happened, talked about my thoughts and worries, and I gave her updates as to how I was feeling on a day-to-day basis.

Catherine was very good at what she did. She was visited by anyone from my company who was dealing with a problem. With her patients, she discussed death, anxiety, layoffs, divorce, and a slew of other everyday problems. She had a diverse range of experience and offered a great perspective on many things. But, what I didn't realize when I first met with her was that a major part of Catherine's job was to help direct her patients to longer-term resources for their problems—to help them find therapists where they could receive more intensive treatments. But because I had an inexperienced view of therapy (thinking my five sessions with Catherine would be adequate) and because I felt strongly about establishing a relationship with only one person, I continued to ignore her suggestion to speak with another therapist.

As time went on I began to realize that my limited sessions with Catherine were not helping me overcome my anxiety. They were a valuable outlet for me, but I was not making forward strides in alleviating my anxiety. I was learning a great deal about myself, my thoughts, and my worries, but due to our limited time, I was not learning the skills necessary and required to overcome my anxiety disorder. I finally took Catherine's advice and agreed to see another therapist. I was skeptical about her initial recommendation to visit *The Mind/Body Medical Institute* because I didn't understand the connection between the mind and body in regard to my anxiety, so I used her other referral for a psychiatrist at Boston Medical Center. It was then that I realized I was heading into uncharted waters—visiting a doctor in an actual hospital.

At my first appointment with my new therapist, we started from the beginning as well. We discussed the details of, at that point, my four-month battle with anxiety. At the end of our first session, she felt the best course of therapy for me would be a combination of cognitive behavioral ("talk") therapy and medication. She wrote a prescription for Paxil and sent me on my way. I left feeling distraught. Taking medication for my anxiety was a whole new ballgame. I knew little about these type of medications (anti-depressants) and wasn't sure that they were necessary for my situation. Because of various stigmas associated with these medications, I had the impression that they changed your personality or made you tired. I didn't want to deal with a medication that changed my personality. I liked who I was, minus this anxiety issue of course. I went home that night and didn't know what to do. I did some research on the internet and soon learned that new medications had come to the market during the previous ten years. These medications, called SSRIs (Selective Serotonin Reuptake Inhibitors) had completely changed the anxiety medication market. They did not affect your attitude, demeanor, or your mood. They were nonaddicting and simply restored the chemical imbalance in the brain which is the catalyst for anxiety. Through my research, the following describes my interpretation of how the medications worked:

> *Your brain sends messages back and forth to your body through your nervous system. These messages are carried by serotonin. When an imbalance of serotonin is present, nerve cells cannot communicate properly with one another. This causes (and enhances) anxiety. A serotonin imbalance can be genetic or it can develop as individuals mature especially when stress is present. Think about a phone line. If each*

time you called your friend's phone and the line was busy, you would never be able to get through to that person. Your brain's messages are the same. In order for you to function properly, these messages need to get through. The more recent SSRI drugs such as Paxil, Zoloft, and others, address the difficulties in communication between nerve cells. They help create a balanced distribution of serotonin between the cells so that your brain can properly communicate with your body. They do not attack your mood or stamina like previous anxiety medications were once thought to do.

The more I read and learned about anxiety and depression medications, the better I felt about them. As I contemplated my decision that night, my good friend from college Jeff called. Jeff was living abroad at the time and called to catch up with me. He asked how I was doing and I masked my problems by telling him that everything was great. I had yet to tell anyone but my immediate family about what I had been going through in regard to anxiety. He filled me in on his life, and as we were about to hang up something came over me. I blurted out a simple question, "Jeff, have you ever had any issues with anxiety?"

Jeff was silent for a moment. This question had come out of the blue so he was a bit taken back I'm sure. After his pause, Jeff answered, "Yes."

Our conversation lasted for another hour. He told me about our senior year of college when he began to have panic attacks in class and experienced severe anxiety on a daily basis. His anxiety led to depression and it eventually got so bad that he almost left school. He finally went to talk to a therapist and spent months battling his disorder. I was completely shocked! I was his best friend in college and had absolutely no idea he was having those issues. He never showed any signs of anxiety and the subject never came up during the eight years since we had graduated. This was further confirmation to me that anxiety was a silent evil.

Jeff elaborated on his past struggles with anxiety and panic attacks, and his weekly therapy. He told me about the medication he was prescribed and the length of time he used it while going through therapy. Eight years ago SSRIs had not yet become available on the market so Jeff was given anxiety medication that typically attacks one's mood and demeanor immediately when ingested. He told me that he used the medication sparingly. In fact, he said that simply knowing he had the medication in his pocket in case of an attack was usually all he needed to avoid having one. He also told me that speaking to a therapist had helped him tremendously.

I then told him about all that I had been going through and I realized how great it felt to have a conversation with someone who had had similar experiences with anxiety and therefore understood all that I was feeling! The conversation would turn out to be a small turning point for me. While it had been extremely helpful to have my parents and sisters supporting me, they had no personal experience with my issues and therefore couldn't offer any advice or substantiate my experiences. Jeff's candid recap of his battle with anxiety was a revelation for me. We traded thoughts, feelings, and symptoms that we had both experienced. For the first time I didn't feel as though I was losing my mind or that I was completely alone. My best friend, who I admired and respected, had been through the same battle.

And more importantly, he had overcome his anxiety and moved past it. Just as we were about to end our conversation, Jeff told me he would dig up the information for the psychiatrist he had seen in Boston and pass it along to me. After we hung up the phone, I felt better than I had in months. I felt comforted and more accepting of what I been feeling and going through.

Two days after our conversation, Jeff sent me his psychiatrist's information. I contacted the doctor that day and learned that he had since retired. His practice was taken over by a colleague of his, and fortunately, the colleague had an immediate opening in his schedule. When I arrived for my appointment later that afternoon, I saw that his office was in the attic of his old, rather dirty, home. He had signs posted from the driveway to the back of the house for patients to follow. When he came downstairs to greet me, we shook hands and I noticed that his grasp seemed weak and frail and that his hands trembled and shook uncontrollably. Right away he seemed a bit odd to me. He was quiet, walked with his head down, and seemed distracted. He led me through his kitchen and up the stairs to the attic. On our way through his home, his small white dog came running at us from another room, jumping and barking in excitement. Before I could even bend down to pet the little guy, the doctor punted him back to his origin and mumbled, "I told you to stay in your basket."

My uneasiness and skepticism grew. As we sat down to begin our session, I saw the man was shaking elsewhere—his legs, arms, and he had an eye twitch. For some reason this unnerved me. He asked me what brought me there and I began to explain my story. But about thirty seconds into my explanation he cut me off and asked me to identify my goal in regard to therapy. I told him I wanted to get over my anxiety and most importantly my attacks. He replied, "You will never get over this anxiety, it's innate and genetic. You can only try to control it and medicate yourself when needed."

He then began describing a few different types of anxiety medication, not the SSRIs that I had read about, but rather intense drugs that attacked your mood, demeanor, and physical body (the same medication prescribed to Jeff ten years prior). He told me that he had been taking drugs like these for years. Could they have been the cause of his constant shaking and trembling? It was at this moment that I realized this doctor was not for me. I was not at all interested in masking my anxiety problem with medication for the rest of my life. I was interested in attacking it head on with a long term solution, not a short term fix. I left the doctor's office immediately and never scheduled a follow-up appointment.

I realized at that moment that finding the right therapist may be a trial and error process. Not every therapist will be the right fit. If you are looking for a therapist, be sure to find a person with whom you are comfortable, and who shares your long-term goals. Also, don't be afraid to change. Even though you may have already invested time with one therapist don't hesitate to start over if need be. There is usually no "quick fix" to a problem so time is on your side. Don't be afraid to find the best therapist for you—the person who will take you the furthest in your recovery—even if it does prolong your recovery time slightly. Fighting anxiety is a battle in which you need to feel confident in and comfortable with your allies. Be certain and choose wisely.

The week following my disappointing appointment, I went back to see my psychiatrist at Boston Medical. I wasn't entirely happy with this psychiatrist either. She seemed extremely overbooked and preoccupied. From her, I never felt as though I'd receive the personal interaction I desired. At that point, I had decided to begin taking medication and agreed to try Paxil. At the same time, I was still in contact with Catherine. She kept telling me about the rave reviews she had been receiving about *The Mind/Body Medical Institute*. With all that I had been through up until that point, I was ready to try almost anything, so I thought to myself, *Why not?*

At *The Mind/Body Medical Institute*, I met a therapist named Janet Fronk. Little did I know at that time that my introduction to Janet would be life-altering. Janet was very pleasant and immediately showed interest in me, my problem, and all that I had to say. I could tell she was well-versed and experienced with anxiety and depression and she immediately made me feel that I was in the right place. She never once looked at her watch and never made me feel like one of her hundreds of patients. She made me feel that I was her only patient and that helping me was her only goal. From our first meeting I knew Janet was the one to help me.

Weeks went by and after each session, I left with more knowledge, understanding, and hope. In fact, anytime I took what I considered to be an extremely valuable tidbit away from a session, I jotted it down onto what turned out to be a small "cheat sheet" of ideas. As my visits to see Janet went on, I became more and more passionate about the "cheat sheet" that I was creating. It listed all the ideas, techniques, and strategies that I considered to be most important and effective in my struggle with anxiety.

About six weeks after I had begun taking Paxil, I noticed a few side effects. I had stomach aches regularly and also started having sexual side effects. Apparently these were common side effects to such medication but were casualties that I was not willing to live with. I knew I needed to try a different medication. Ironically, just after I had made that decision, I ran into a good friend, Shane. We made small talk for a while and then I told him about my anxiety, some of the things I had been through, and my most recent reaction to the Paxil. To my surprise, he shared his story which was very similar to mine.

Shane was a few years older than me and our lifestyles and personalities were very similar. He said that when he was my age (close to turning thirty) he also went through a very difficult time, perhaps his own quarter-life crisis. He developed anxiety and had trouble sleeping, eating, and working out. Shane eventually became depressed. He started taking Paxil and had the same side effects that I did. So he tried three other medications before finally landing on Zoloft. He felt that Zoloft worked best for him because it helped him control his anxiety while not producing the side effects that other medications had. Finding the right medication is difficult because the side effects can differ from person to person. The varying genetic make-ups of people can cause one medication to be good for one person while not for another, and vice versa. Shane went on to tell me that after switching medications he began to make even more progress battling his anxiety disorder. It was another extremely important conversation with a close friend. What struck me most was the understanding that finding the right medication is also a trial and error process much like finding the right therapist.

At my next session with Janet we discussed a medication switch from Paxil to Zoloft. She supported my decision and further explained the purpose of these medications—they are intended to help you control your physical anxiety which then allows you to deal with the thoughts that cause your anxious moments. My good friend's father, Dr. McGinn, is a psychologist and also explained how to view the medication:

> *Imagine your anxious mind as a train that rests in the train station. As your anxiety grows and you develop an anxiety disorder, the train begins to pull away from the station. Soon you realize this train is going full steam ahead and there is no stopping it. SSRI medications help bring that train back*

in the station so you can better physically relax while you work out the stressors and thoughts that are troubling you. The medications help you address your problems without having to worry about the physical symptoms of anxiety—physical symptoms which quite often take on a life of their own.

Months went by and I would meet with Janet once every week. I'd have good days and bad days, a good week and then a bad week. I constantly teeter tottered between good and bad. Just when I thought I had started to "turn the corner", I'd revert back to my old way of thinking and the way I used to feel. I tried not to get frustrated with the up and down progress but it was tough for me to be patient because in my life previously I had been able to get results rather quickly. However, I would try and focus on the fact that recovery takes time and I'd try to enjoy the ups and manage through the downs. Most importantly, I didn't let my down days keep me down. I knew that each day would be a fresh start and I'd do my best to think of each day as independent of the previous day. If I had a bad Monday, I didn't carry those negative thoughts into Tuesday. I'd simply start over and start new!

I truly owe my progress, and ultimate recovery, to Janet. She is not only an excellent therapist but she was the right therapist and the right fit for me. Although my road to finding her may have included a few setbacks, in hindsight it was well worth the journey. I am convinced that without Janet's help and education I would not be where I am today and for that I am grateful. My finding Janet reinforces the importance of finding the right therapist. For your own journey, the best advice I can offer is to seek out a therapist who specializes in what you are struggling with. If anxiety is your problem, find a therapist with an expertise in anxiety. If you need help with depression, seek a therapist who specializes in depression. You wouldn't hire an electrician to come to your home to fix a leaky sink. As you know, people are sought after based on their training and expertise. Finding the right therapist for your troubles is no different.

It's actually quite fitting that I am writing this chapter tonight. It is one o'clock in the morning, about eleven months to the day from when anxiety first blindsided me. I came home tonight from my last appointment with Janet Fronk. In the past three months, I have truly turned a corner and tonight Janet and I had our final session together. As I left her office, she wished me well and congratulated me. She explained that she was proud of me for all that I had accomplished—seeking her out, committing to our sessions, and following my therapy through until the end. Our conversation reminded me of a similar conversation I had had with my oldest sister months prior.

When my oldest sister first found out about my issues with anxiety she called me on the phone. As we spoke about what I was going through we talked a little about the therapy I was about to partake in. She told me she was so proud of me for being a "man". I remember pausing and asking her what she meant. She said that it takes a real man to identify when he needs help and to then do something about it. She said that most men would continue to struggle, trying to fix things on their own while continuing to live in misery. She reiterated how proud of me she was and how mature she viewed my decision to seek help. Whether you're a man or a woman it doesn't matter. It takes a very strong person to be honest with him or herself and to seek help. Overlooking the negative stigma attached to therapy and overcoming any potential embarrassment related to your problems takes strength and fortitude.

And with strength also comes reward. While being strong might mean choosing a riskier option, that option is usually the one with the potential for the greatest reward. In regard to anxiety, not addressing your problems or hiding them might seem to be the easier option to choose. And if you choose that path, you might be able to live your life for a while, dodging and hiding your problems. But somewhere down the road, I am confident that those problems will rear their ugly heads and cause you great strife. On the other hand, you could choose the riskier option—confront and fight your anxiety head on. This was the path that I chose and I can assure you it has been a difficult journey. But, it has proven to be the most rewarding and beneficial. It has given me the strength, knowledge, and peace that I so desperately yearned for. And my decision to share with the world my personal feelings and struggle with anxiety in this book only solidifies the fact that I view myself as a strong person who made the right choice. I am no longer worried about the stigmas associated with anxiety, anxiety disorders, or even depression. I am not ashamed of who I am or what I went through and never again will I dream of changing places with another person.

8

What Led to My Quarter-Life Crisis

By battling my anxiety disorder head on, I had the chance to examine the thoughts and expectations in both my personal and professional lives that created my anxiety and led to my quarter-life crisis. At age twenty-nine, there were many changes going on in my life and I had allowed stress and anxiety to build and fester inside of me. This was dangerous because stress can heighten your body's awareness and reactions towards anxiety and can put your body on alert for trouble until one day a trigger brings it all to the forefront. I had no idea I was leading myself down this unhealthy path until the Boston terror threat capitalized on my heightened state of anxiety and triggered my first panic attack.

So what caused my build up of stress and anxiety? To determine this, I looked back at my life. At the age of twenty-seven, after having lived in Boston for five years, I received a promotion and the opportunity to move to New York City where I would spend two years on a work assignment. It was perfect timing for me—I was single, career focused, and financially stable enough to enjoy New York City. The position was a stepping stone to bigger and better things within my company. The plan was to work hard in New York for a short time and then move back to our company's headquarters in Boston with a new role and increased responsibilities. The job in New York also allowed me to work from my apartment which provided me with great freedom as I wasn't strapped to a desk all day long. I was very excited and upon moving to New York, I developed a *worry about it later* attitude and lived day to day with little responsibility other than my job. I thought I could avoid "adult responsibilities"—mortgage payments, providing for a family, relationship commitments, being tied to an office—until I moved back to Boston. I was thrilled to have the opportunity to live in a different city and experience new things.

My two years in New York City were everything I had hoped they would be. I had a fantastic time, made great friends, and enjoyed working from my home office. But somehow during my time there I developed the thought that once I moved back to Boston, I'd need to "grow up". That meant maturing, settling down, possibly even starting a family. (Mind you, I wasn't even dating anyone seriously at that time!) I began to imagine myself in my father's shoes—being a husband, father, and a responsible provider—and then tried to figure out whether I'd be happy in that role at that point in my life. Essentially the move back to Boston meant a new life and a new *me*.

Looking back even earlier, I believe this worry stemmed from my childhood. When I was young, my family would take a vacation to Cape Cod every summer. My mother, father, two sisters and I would stay at a hotel in Hyannis. My father was a tax accountant, so while we were there he would spend the week working for the hotel, and in return, the hotel would give our family a complimentary week's stay. My father would work his regular office hours while my mother looked after us. Our day consisted of sleeping late, eating, playing in the pool, and watching TV. While we enjoyed ourselves my father would wake up early, put on his suit and tie, and walk down to the end of the hall to the office the hotel provided for him. My sisters and I would race back and forth from our room to the pool, each time stopping at the door to my father's office to yell in, "Hi Dad!"

You'd think after doing this eight to ten times each day my father would have asked us to stop. But each time he'd pause, smile, and say hello back to us. Then he'd put his head back down and continue working. It was a prime example of what a hard worker my father was (and still is). Because of this, whenever I thought about growing up I pictured myself in my father's position. I started to wonder, had he enjoyed himself? Would I if I assumed that role? No longer was I the carefree boy running around having fun all day. I felt I needed to start being the man who supported his family. But at the same time, those responsibilities scared me—especially the financial ones. Was I really ready for that? Would I be good at it? I had grown so accustomed to being "the kid" that the thought of maturing into the "responsible adult" challenged my thoughts of future happiness. Like many of my peers, I had spent the majority of my twenties on my own—single, independent, and focused solely on myself. I worried that I had developed a more selfish attitude compared to that of my father and I wondered how I'd know when I needed to make that transition from child to responsible adult.

I started to put so much pressure on myself to become that responsible person that I began to lose sight of my present life. My mind raced with images of me working in that hotel office in Hyannis. The images reminded me of many other summer days at my home in Connecticut—my sisters and I swimming in our backyard pool all day long while my dad called from his office to check on us and my mother. Again, my father working while we enjoyed the luxuries that he provided for us. He worked hard each and every day to give us the best he possibly could, including a mother who could stay home to care for her children. These thoughts began to consume my mind as my two year assignment in New York City slowly came to an end. I anticipated my move back to Boston, where I thought I would *grow up* and become a responsible man much like my father.

Soon the day came when the job I had always wanted opened up in Boston. I couldn't believe what a perfect fit it was, the managerial position that I wanted, at the level I had hoped for, in the city to which I wanted to return. I applied for the job immediately. The hiring Director was a mentor of mine and we had kept in touch religiously throughout my time in New York. He called me about the job and agreed that while it would be a great fit, there would be many applicants for the job who were older and more experienced than I was at the time. He agreed that I had done well in New York and deserved a promotion, so he served up an alternative—a different job managing our largest account. This was also a fantastic opportunity but would unfortunately require me to relocate to Arkansas. That move was not one that I was interested in making. I reiterated that I wanted the job in Boston. A few heated discussions later, he began to understand and even validated my concerns about the position and the move to Arkansas, yet he still didn't agree to hire me for the Boston job that I so desperately wanted.

Two weeks later I again got a call from the Director. He had *another* job opening, this time managing our second biggest account. This position also required a relocation, this time to Minneapolis. Unfortunately for me, I wasn't interested in moving anywhere at that time but back home to Boston. Our discussion became even more heated. The Director felt strongly that I should take one of the two positions he had offered and that I should have been grateful for them. And while I was extremely appreciative, I felt he should have listened more to my career aspirations, not solely think about helping himself by having me take one of the positions he needed to fill. He abruptly, and rather unprofessionally ended the phone call with a snide remark and told me I'd be sorry for not jumping at either of the two opportunities he had recommended.

Over the course of the few weeks that followed, I was stressed like never before. Not only did I think I would never get the job I really wanted, but I also started to fear that I wouldn't get promoted at all. I even thought about looking for a new job with a different company. And just when I thought it was as bad as it could have been, the Director made it worse by lying to his counterparts. Typical protocol for discussing job opportunities required the hiring Director to first ask permission from the perspective applicant's current boss. When it became clear that we had been having job conversations, my boss and her boss blew up, and asked who had contacted whom. He never admitted to having been the one to call me first, or offering the two jobs that required relocation. He left me in a very uncomfortable predicament with my own boss and her superiors.

I felt my chances of getting back to Boston had become hopeless and that the career I had spent years working so hard to build had been put in jeopardy. I didn't want to leave my company, but I started to think that it might be my only option. Weeks went by and I heard nothing from the hiring Director. Finally, I got a call from my boss who told me that there had been a turn of events and that the Director would be contacting me shortly to discuss the managerial position I wanted in Boston. I was relieved and elated later that afternoon when I spoke with the Director and he told me that even with the sizeable number of applicants, I was one of the best candidates for the job. He never made any reference to our prior disagreements and spoke only about the opportunity in Boston. He told me that his hesitancy in hiring me had to do with my age because if hired, I'd be one of the youngest managers at my company. He worried about backlash from colleagues and human resources, and about putting himself on the line if he hired me. He explained that if I was hired for the job, I'd need to "look, act, and play the part." He told me that all eyes would be on me and that I'd need to be the type of person who lived for his job. As I assured him that I was his man, I became concerned with his description of how I'd need to act. I have always worked hard, but I've also enjoyed my life and made sure to keep a balance between my professional and personal lives. I was not the kind of person who lived for his job only.

Regardless, it was the job that I wanted and it would get me back to Boston. A few weeks later, I was officially offered the job and I happily accepted. Unbeknownst to me I took the baggage from my recent professional turmoil and the pressure the Director had put on me back to Boston. These issues, thoughts, and pressures only added to the personal stress I had placed on myself at that time to become a more responsible and mature person upon returning home.

When I moved back to Boston, I left what became a very comfortable and enjoyable lifestyle in New York City, and a fantastic group of friends. I didn't realize how much I'd miss them until I arrived in Boston and found that many of my old friends had married and moved out to the suburbs of Boston. This transition highlighted the fact that I was twenty-nine years old, single, and starting all over . . . again. And it seemed as though the older I got, the more difficult it had become to uproot myself and start fresh.

This difficulty, coupled with my iceberg belief[1] that I had always thought I'd be married by age thirty, caused me to feel that something was off, almost as if I was *behind* in life.

My first day in the new job came quickly and I was excited to get back to Boston and back into the office. During my first few weeks on the job I became fixated on learning everything that I possibly could, many days working extremely long hours. I put so much pressure on myself to do not just a good job, but a great job, that I lost sight of many things that I had once enjoyed. During those first weeks, I spent every Friday working until ten o'clock at night. By the time I would finally leave the office I'd have just enough energy to eat a quick dinner before collapsing into bed. As if working long and hard didn't create enough stress, my company also released a major announcement during those first few weeks in my new assignment—they had been acquired and our jobs,

---

[1] Iceberg belief – Belief in your own mind that on the surface seems like a small thought but in reality has much more substance to it (under the surface). This belief is typically formed throughout years of experiences, upbringing, and childhood thoughts and events. It is based on thoughts and beliefs you have built (many times subconsciously) and typically is the main reason why you react the way you do today.

careers, and futures were all uncertain and unsafe. My anxiety was growing and growing.

Also, as I began to settle into my new position, I learned that the majority of my colleagues were older than I. Most were married, had families, and owned beautiful homes. As the only one who was single, I'd spend most lunches and breaks listening to them talk about their children, their husbands and wives, and what they did on the weekends. It seemed to me that most of them made it all sound so lifeless and mundane that I began to worry. I would look around my office and wonder if that was all life had to offer— arriving at work everyday at seven in the morning, returning home at seven at night, and getting up to do it all over again the following day. It didn't seem all that appealing to me. I'd look at the President of our company and wonder if he was happy working all day, six days a week, only to head home just in time to kiss his three young children good night before they headed off to sleep. Two minutes with his children after spending all day in the office just didn't seem right. Going to work, heading home to a spouse, taking care of kids, paying bills, weekend barbecues with neighbors, and trips to Home Depot and the supermarket—were they going to be enough to make me content?

I suddenly became confused. These things were always what I had strived for, what I thought I had wanted. Growing up in a typical, happy family, it had become etched in my mind that I'd live my life the same way my parents had and that would make me content. Compared to the timeline they had created—marrying at a young age and having children right away—I was *behind* and I began to think about this constantly. I wasn't ready for a wife or family, yet I was almost thirty years old. Would I ever be ready? I moved back to Boston to settle down, yet the thought of settling down frightened me. I felt trapped. I never bothered to think that the evolution of a person might take more time. I expected to become this vastly different person once I arrived in Boston, and when it didn't happen I became anxious and upset with myself. My anxiety continued to grow.

While struggling with the idea of being a husband and father, I also worried about not having someone to love. I believe that this worry developed from my previous relationship. When I was younger, just out of college, my girlfriend of four years and I broke up. She was my first love and in my fairy tale life the only girl that I would ever love. For many years I thought she would one day be my wife and the mother of my children. Because of this notion, for years, I couldn't get over her. After we broke up I felt as though I had lost a part of my heart and that the rest of my life would be forever tainted. This worry weighed on the back of my mind for quite sometime. I felt that I wouldn't ever love someone else the way I once loved this girl, and that being in a relationship with a different person would always be a compromise. This added to my anxiety as I strived to find love and fulfillment with another person. Perhaps I viewed being married, going to work each day, and heading home to a family each night as mundane because I never thought I'd have a spouse to love as completely as I did my college girlfriend. I felt I wouldn't have a spouse who would make all of those things worthwhile, even exciting. I pictured my future without the love that I thought I needed to make me happy and content for the rest of my life.

I share this with you for two reasons. First, to show you that my loss of love was an anxiety-producing event for me. And second, to provide you with a prime example of how our own over thinking can add to our stress levels and anxiety. I was the one who created my anxiety by perceiving something so definitively. How could I have worried that my only potential for true love had come and gone by age twenty-two? In regard to anxiety, I have learned that it is not necessarily what causes your anxiety that is important but rather how you perceive and manage that anxiety. Unfortunately I didn't always know this and unbeknownst to me at that time my first panic attack was only a few short weeks away.

By the way, I did eventually meet and fall in love with the girl that I will some day marry. She's everything I had been looking and waiting for and what we have together shows me all that wasn't right with my first love. Many of us hold onto our first loves because of the connection we shared and the desire we had to never let that person go. But many times that emotion and desire can cloud our judgment about what is best for us. It took time, and the introduction to my future wife, to understand that my first love and I just weren't right for each other, regardless of how much we cared for one another. Eventually I was able to let go of the thought that I may have lost something irreplaceable.

9

Fueling my Quarter-Life Crisis

In addition to all of the stressors that spurred my quarter-life crisis, there was one other circumstance that played a large part in my struggle: I had *arrived*. Simply explained, I had checked off all of the major goals that I had set for myself and had arrived at my "destination". Up until that point my life had been a series of setting, striving, and accomplishing goals. From these goals I derived motivation. They were what I worked towards and pursued each day.

So what happens when you accomplish all of your goals, when you reach your destination? What happens when you *arrive?* Well, the answer lies in the type of goals that you set. Through my struggles I have come to realize that there are two types of goals, those that can be viewed as tangible destination goals and those that can be viewed as ways to live your life. While setting destination goals can provide a great deal of motivation, achieving them can also lead to unexplained anxiety and/or depression. On the other hand, when goals are set in regard to how you live your life, there is no box to check off and no trophy to take home, simply a guiding reminder of what you consider to be valuable in your life. These goals can be pursued each and every day.

A good family friend of mine, Bridget, is dealing with the difficulties of achieving tangible destination goals. Bridget had set specific destination goals in her life: she hoped to find a kind, loving spouse, she wanted a happy and successful marriage, she wished for financial stability, and more than anything Bridget hoped to become a mother. And one-by-one, Bridget began checking off these tangible destination goals. She found an incredible husband, has been married for over five years, and she and her husband have reached a point where they are financially stable and secure. What's even more amazing is that after a long difficult road with many failed attempts, Bridget finally became a mother to a healthy, beautiful baby boy. Bridget had not been expected to ever be able to give birth, so the conception and delivery of her son was truly a miracle. Bridget had achieved everything that she had hoped for in her life. In fact, Bridget admits that her life is absolutely perfect—there is nothing more she could ask for. So it's surprising to learn that Bridget suffers from anxiety and depression. She has been taking Zoloft for over a year now and has no idea why she has anxious and depressing thoughts and feelings when her life has far exceeded her expectations. Sometimes she gets so frustrated and depressed that she doesn't want to get out of bed in the morning.

In my opinion, by achieving these tangible goals, Bridget has *arrived* at her destination and lacks a new, clear set of goals that would continue to drive her forward. Just as I felt after I had achieved all my major goals—I graduated college, bought my first home, ran a marathon, got my new dream job, and was living in Boston—I had also *arrived*. And what was most distressing was that I lacked the foresight to create new goals, refocus, and commit myself to those new goals. Even when it became apparent to me that I needed a new set of goals, nothing jumped out at me. I pushed so hard for so long to achieve all that I had set out to achieve that I never stopped to think about what I would do once I got to where I wanted to be. The journey to achieve my goals became my life and once I arrived I had no idea what to do from there. Similar to the cartoon that illustrates the donkey always moving forward trying to reach the carrot dangling in front of him—did you ever notice that the donkey never gets the carrot? If he did, wouldn't he stop galloping, sit down, and eat the carrot? What would motivate him to keep trekking across the desert? Once I arrived, and ate my carrot, I lost a sense of myself and my purpose. I lost my daily motivation. That is the danger of creating only tangible destination goals.

Today I am recommitted to life and a new set of goals; goals that are very different from those I recently checked off. They are no longer tangible destination goals, they are a way of being and a way of living. Most importantly, they are goals that can be continually pursued rather than achieved, checked off, and dropped from my list completely. The following are my current goals in life:

1) Live anxiety and depression free
2) Enjoy the moment and worry less about the future
3) Enjoy what I have
4) Slow down...simmer
5) Be happy with myself
6) Control my thoughts
7) Life does not have a blueprint, there is no rulebook to follow nor any way to keep score (so don't live like it does)
8) Write and publish this book

As you can see, most of these goals are much different from the tangible destination goals I had set many years ago. In fact, the person I was previously probably wouldn't be motivated by the goals that I have created for myself today. But I've changed. My goals have changed. With these new goals, no longer do I hope to one day check them off my list. I now hope to use them as guiding principles in my daily life. With these goals there is no arriving, only living.

10

The Cheat Sheet

One sunny, unseasonably warm Sunday in November I met a close friend for brunch. It was a spectacular day—sunny and warm with a slight breeze. My friend Lane and I were sitting on the patio of one of my favorite little cafes in New York City. I was in extremely high spirits, excited not only for the beautiful day ahead but also because I felt as though I had truly turned a corner in my struggle with my anxiety disorder. No longer did I feel constantly worried about having an anxiety attack. I began to view my future as I always had; promising, happy, and full of anxiety-free moments. Very simply, my anxiety no longer controlled me. Yet in the midst of my happiness, I realized that Lane wasn't quite herself. It hadn't been noticeable to me at first but as we sat, talked, and waited for our food, I realized that she didn't seem to be her usual cheerful, care-free self.

I questioned her about this and we soon found ourselves involved in a serious conversation about life's stressors, uncertainties, and anxiety. At that point, Lane knew that I had been going through some difficult things but I had yet to confide in her completely. And so I started from the beginning—describing my first frightening attack that horrible January day ten months earlier. I explained to her all that I had been through and more importantly all that I had learned from my struggles. I told her about therapy, medication, and the skills needed to combat anxiety. Then, I thought of the little "cheat sheet" I had made for myself and kept in my wallet. I thought it might contain some valuable insight for Lane in regard to what she was feeling. I shared it with her, reading each point and explaining what each meant to me.

Lane loved my cheat sheet. She started jotting down my fifteen points making her own little cheat sheet so that she would have reminders to carry around with her. A few days later Lane called and told me how much better she was feeling from our talk, and most importantly, from my cheat sheet. She told me how much she liked each point and how she had been able to focus on many of them in just a short time. Our conversation that afternoon was not only eye opening for Lane, but also life changing. It pointed her in the right direction and gave her strategies to practice and goals to strive for. Although it wasn't the end all in Lane's turnaround and battle with anxiety, I was pleasantly surprised by how much my cheat sheet had helped her, especially in such a short time. I knew how valuable these thoughts were for me, but up until that point I never realized how helpful they could be for others. The strategies and thoughts on my cheat sheet had now become such a natural part of my thinking I hadn't thought of looking at them from someone else's perspective. I soon realized that this cheat sheet could help many others in addition to Lane, and so I began writing this book.

During my struggle with anxiety, I found myself looking at my cheat sheet whenever I had time on my hands—sitting on a plane, in a meeting, at my desk, even at home. Sometimes I just found this cheat sheet useful in simply distracting my mind when I needed a diversion. You might find other ways to use the cheat sheet. Regardless, I hope you find these strategies and thoughts as helpful as I did. They sprang from the several months I spent in therapy, from my research about anxiety, and from conversations with family and friends.

(1) **Breathe, relax, and slow down**

Taking deep conscious breaths is extremely important. Your breath is what signals to your body whether there is trouble looming or not. Deep, slow, relaxed breaths tell your body that you are calm and centered and that everything is alright. When you get scared, nervous, and/or stressed you tend to hold your breath. This sends signals to your body that things are not alright and your body will react accordingly. By taking a deep breath periodically throughout the day, and especially when you are feeling anxious, you let your mind and body know that all is well and you can begin to calm down.

Panic attacks are caused by lack of oxygen. Breathing properly—consistently and deeply—can help prevent panic attacks. It is when you begin to focus on panicking and allow this fear to impact your normal breathing that an attack may occur. When you begin to get anxious your body will begin to take short quick breaths rather than long deep breaths. This sends a signal throughout your body that something is wrong and your anxiety will continue to build. As your anxiety builds typically your body will search for a release, potentially an anxiety or panic attack. Taking deep breaths at the onset of these anxious feelings can be a valuable tool to assist you in avoiding anxiety or panic attacks altogether.

My therapist actually gave me small blue circular stickers to attach all around my office, home, and car. The stickers were meant to be reminders for me to stop what I was doing, focus on my breathing, and take a long, deep, relaxing breath. When I first began practicing this it felt strange and awkward. But I continued to practice and each time I saw a blue dot I automatically took a deep relaxing breath. Immediately, I would begin to feel better. Today I don't even need to see a blue sticker. This technique was so effective at training my body to periodically take deep relaxing breaths that I do it almost subconsciously now throughout my day. Also, in anxious situations, I now find myself reacting to feelings and symptoms of anxiety with deep breaths, never giving my anxiety a chance to grow. Whether in an anxious situation or not, with each deep breath I feel more calm, more focused, and centered. Breathing correctly is essential and has been an amazing discovery in my battle with anxiety.

In addition to long, deep, relaxing breaths, I can't emphasize enough how important it is to slow yourself down. If you are anything like me, you most likely run around all day trying to get everything done that has found its way onto your "to-do" list. By making a conscious effort to slow yourself down and take a more relaxed approach to daily activities, you will not only give your mind and body a calmer overall feeling, but you will create a more centered and relaxed internal structure that will most likely lead to a happier and healthier spirit. Remember, everything *will* get done. Simply allow yourself the time to do it.

I was speaking with a close friend recently who is a prime example of someone who needs to slow down, relax, and breathe. At the time of our conversation, she was well aware of all I had been dealing with in regard to anxiety and had also experienced moderate bouts with anxiety herself. She is a very intelligent, successful, and caring person. She holds two degrees (one from Harvard) and is a person who will succeed in anything she puts her mind to.

She began telling me about her previous day, a Sunday, where she had had no set plans and had been excited for a day to do whatever she wanted. My friend made a list of "to-dos" and set out! She started by shopping at some of her favorite places. While walking around, on what should have been a very leisurely day, she actually began to unknowingly rush from store to store. In fact, she rushed through her entire "to-do" list until it was completed. All she could think about was *finishing* the next item on her list. Even after she arrived home she rushed around the kitchen throwing together her dinner and then rushed into her living room and scarfed down her food with haste. Finally, she sat back and just stopped. It was at that moment that she realized what she had been doing the entire day—rushing. For no reason at all, she had spent her entire day tense, rushed, and stressed. She had nothing pressing to do, nor any deadlines or people to meet, yet she ran around all day, full of anxiety, trying to get everything done. And for what reason?

We agreed that in the future she needed to do a better job of identifying when she was rushing, and to then try and manage that behavior by taking deep, relaxing breaths and slowing down. She could have enjoyed herself much more that Sunday if she had focused on the present moment, or task, while she completed it. The end result wouldn't have changed. She could have finished everything on her list timely and successfully. More importantly, her enjoyment in doing them would not have been tainted, it would have been increased. So next time you feel yourself rushing for no apparent reason, slow down! The joy should be in the journey and not solely in the completion.

(2) TODAY – Live for today and be present

Living for today only and being present has never had such clarity as it does to me today. When my therapist first introduced this concept to me, it seemed completely foreign. *Be present?* It might seem like a simple term but I really had no idea what it meant. My therapist defined it as the concentrated effort to focus on things that are happening in the present moment. She told me that being present can be as easy as taking your mind off of a particular worry and focusing it on your moving feet as you walk down the street. After my initial introduction to this idea I was still somewhat skeptical, but as I practiced interrupting my thoughts with "present mindfulness" I began to understand its benefits. Being present helped decrease the amount of time I spent worrying about my future and my anxiety disorder. It also interrupted what I consider to be the *circle of doom*: negative thoughts that feed off one another and send your mind into a whirlwind of hopelessness and self-defeat.

I practiced mindfulness by acknowledging to myself when I was thinking about the future and then immediately pulling my mind off of that thought and refocusing it on something else in the present moment. Many times I did this by simply focusing on my feet as they hit the ground while I was walking. Other times I admired trees, birds, or the weather if I was outside. If I was driving I would focus on other car's license plates, reading their letters and numbers to myself. There were so many miniscule things that I used to interrupt the compulsive thoughts and scenarios on which I tended to dwell. I used these things to turn my focus to the present moment. At first it felt almost impossible and I could only focus on the present moment for seconds at a time. But with practice, patience, and perseverance it became much easier to me and I was slowly able to extend the length of my present thinking. Today, being present has become almost second nature.

Living for *today* and in the moment can change your life. One way to practice this is to pick out a ritual or routine that you do everyday by yourself. I chose brushing my teeth. Each morning when I woke up and brushed my teeth I practiced being in the moment. Prior to practicing present mindfulness, I would use that time to let my mind wander about the day ahead of me, the night before, or even things that might happen weeks, months, years down the road. But with my newfound awareness, I would focus on the present moment of cleaning my teeth—feeling the bristles of the toothbrush scrubbing each of my teeth, tasting the minty toothpaste, and watching in the mirror as the head of the toothbrush moved around my mouth. I tried not to allow my mind to wander and kept it focused on the present moment, brushing my teeth. If my mind did wander, I acknowledged this and gently brought my attention and focus back to my teeth and the present moment. Today when I brush my teeth, I don't have to work so hard at being present or practicing mindfulness. It comes easier than it did when I first started. My practice has paid off and it's now natural for me to be present when brushing my teeth.

(3) **Stop future thinking—don't get bogged down with *'what ifs'* and *'shoulds'***

This strategy works hand in hand with practicing present mindfulness. Future thinking is the number one producer of anxiety. Learning to control your future thinking, your thoughts about your future, will ultimately allow you to control your anxiety. One controls his or her future thinking by being present. When your mind is entrenched in the present moment it is impossible to simultaneously worry about the future. That's the beauty of your mind. Although it has amazing power and limitless potential, the one thing it cannot do is think about two things at once. And for that we are fortunate. If you can train your mind to focus on the present moment more often, you will eliminate the bad habit of future thinking of which many of us are guilty. More importantly, if you can control your mind, you can control your happiness and the way you feel.

I'm not saying that all future thinking is bad. It is important for you to plan for your future, and many times the day ahead of you. It's productive and beneficial to do so. In fact, I live by an important saying—*plan for tomorrow, yet live for today.* But to do this effectively, one must also be mindful. It's the *worrying* about the future that can cause harm. When you find yourself obsessing over something that may or may not come to fruition, it's important to immediately cease that thought and bring your mind back to the present moment. This takes practice and sometimes five seconds after you do this your mind will jump right back to where you were. Don't get frustrated. Be easy on yourself. Simply notice this and gently take control of your thoughts again. Keep practicing and before you know it you will have your mind conditioned to focus on the present moment almost subconsciously.

This has helped me tremendously. All of my life I have been a planner and a future thinker. In fact, as far back as I can remember I have always focused on the future—things I wanted from life, what I wanted to achieve—never realizing that I should really have been focused on the present moment. Growing up I always had the impression that everything I did before I settled down and got married was simply in preparation for that future life. Perhaps this had to do with how I was raised, the way society portrays marriage, or even the experiences I had growing up with parents who have been together for almost forty years.

Whatever the reason, I had a hidden belief, an iceberg belief that my life didn't really begin until I was married and started my own family. I thought that by age thirty I would be there. Heck, I thought by age twenty-five I would be there. I never realized that this belief had huge ramifications on the way I lived my life. It forced me to live in anticipation of that time rather than live in the moment. I was letting my life pass me by.

I can recall in high school anticipating where I would go to college. In college, I anticipated and worried about what I would do in the *real world*. After college, I thought about my career and where it would lead. And over the last few years leading up to my anxiety, my quarter-life crisis, I spent an inordinate amount of time worrying about many future circumstances and events. I thought about my professional path, if and when I would get married, who I would marry, if I would truly love her, and whether or not my career and a family would make me happy and content. Once I developed my anxiety disorder, my tendency to future think only compounded my anxiety and drove me deeper into an anxiety disorder and moderate depression. I even began to imagine myself battling anxiety itself for years to come! I never saw the light at the end of the tunnel. It wasn't until I acquired the skill to stop my future thinking and worrying that I began to overcome my battle with anxiety. There is a lot to be said for learning how to enjoy the moment.

I have found that when attempting to change your mind's focus there are a few words that you should red flag—*what if, should*, and *should not*. Many of my anxious worries started with the phrase *what if*. It focuses your mind on something that has yet to happen, usually something that you are dreadfully anticipating. More importantly, it typically represents something that may *never* happen, something that is not a definitive. The moment you start a sentence with *what if*, train yourself to stop right there—don't finish that statement! It is rarely, if ever, followed by a healthy or productive thought. *What if I die tomorrow? What if I never get married? What if I never find happiness? What if I don't get that job? What if I get divorced one day? What if I have another panic or anxiety attack?* The list can go on and on. When you find yourself starting a sentence with *what if*, try to stop yourself from completing it. If you can, great! If not, realize that what you are worrying about is not worth your time and energy and try not to give it too much life in your mind. *What if* statements can only produce anxiety when given credibility in your mind.

Now if you find yourself having trouble halting your thoughts, that your mind typically finishes *what if* scenarios, try another technique—turn each *what if* into a positive statement. Have fun with it if you can! Rather than, *what if I don't get that job*, try *what if I DO get that job?!* Instead of, *what if I die tomorrow*, try *what if I LIVE tomorrow?!* Think about it. What would you do with your day? If you live, that's where you have decisions to make and thoughts to consider. Why should you waste your precious time and energy on worrying about negatives that may never come to fruition, especially thoughts that are counterproductive to your happiness? Turn them into positives and be grateful!

Should and *should not* are other words to red flag. Many times in my sessions with my therapist I found myself saying things like *I shouldn't feel this way, I should not be anxious in a meeting or in church,* or even *I should be stronger and not fear anxiety.* Just like the *what ifs*, these *shoulds* are not healthy or productive statements. Who determines what or how you should feel? Who says that you shouldn't feel anxious in a meeting? It's not productive to think that you should or should not feel a certain way because of certain expectations you may have forced upon yourself. When Janet Fronk, asked me *who determines how you should feel,* my answer was "me". When I answered she raised her eyebrow as if to hint that I was incorrect. She then explained that there is no particular way that I should feel. Somewhere along the line I subconsciously determined how I thought I should act and feel in certain situations and this became the standard to which I held myself. I put pressure and stress on myself to be this certain person. I think most of us do this. Rather than simply take each event and reaction as it came, I felt I *should* have reacted to various circumstances in a way that I had subconsciously imagined and strived to do. Believing that I should have felt a certain way was my initial error. *Should, should not,* and *what if* statements are the equivalent to sparks that start a fire. Extinguishing this spark before it can ignite a larger fire is the key to controlling your thoughts and future worries. You can't have a fire without a spark.

(4) <u>Identify and control your negative thinking</u>

The goal with this strategy is to be able to eventually change and control your thoughts without much effort or strain, similar to the way your natural thought process flows. This technique requires continuous and committed practice so that one day it will become second nature to you. It's like the first time you picked up a golf club and began to play. Perhaps you took a lesson? If you didn't, I'm sure your first time out was atrocious. If you did, most likely you were taught to focus on the details of your swing—the position of your hands, your wrists, the level of your shoulders, and keeping your head down. These things probably seemed foreign to you initially but with much practice and commitment, you slowly decreased your constant need to focus on such minute details. You trained your mind and body (your hands, wrists, shoulders, and head) as to what needed to be done in order to swing successfully. Once these actions became subconscious and second nature you could then begin to focus on the bigger picture—the ball.

I was never taught how to control my thoughts—how to identify negative thoughts and prevent myself from focusing on them. In fact, I lived my life under the impression that my thoughts controlled me. I never monitored my thoughts, whatever thoughts came to me (good or bad) I allowed them to remain and essentially gave them life. My thoughts were simply what they were and my reaction to them was just who I was— right?! Yet only part of this is true. Yes, you might react to situations and events based on your personality and the thought processes you've developed over the course of your life. But, this is not necessarily who you have to be, how you have to think, or how you have to react. You can transform the way you think and react and the way your thoughts affect you by taking control of everything that enters your mind. By monitoring what you allow your mind to spend time thinking about, you can have a tremendously positive impact on your overall well-being, demeanor, and your life.

Negative thoughts can come in many shapes and forms. Often in this book you've heard me talk about future thoughts as negative thoughts, but many times negative thoughts can involve dwelling on the past or thinking about the present as well. Regardless of the origin of your thoughts, identifying them as negative, and then changing your focus are essential components of avoiding negative thinking.

Take, for example, an acquaintance of mine named Buckley—a twenty-eight year old woman who lives in New York City. She is healthy, successful, and has a great group of friends who she enjoys on a daily basis. But, Buckley's mother has cancer and she is dying. Within the last year Buckley has turned to alcohol, drugs, and other unhealthy habits to try and cope with the eventual loss of her mother. She feels that this situation is extremely unfair and has let it sway her from her nice, sweet demeanor. She has actually become rude, obnoxious, and quite sarcastic. It's understandable that Buckley would grieve and deal with this tragic circumstance in many different ways but she has allowed this situation to completely infiltrate her life. It has changed the person she has been for twenty-seven years and, more importantly, the person her mother had raised her to be. In addition, her constant focus on this present day tragedy has driven her into depression and caused her to have frequent bouts with anxiety.

I hope Buckley will soon find a way to control her thoughts so that she is not constantly focusing on only the negatives in her life. I hope she discovers a way to grieve and deal with this situation in a way that will allow her to find herself once again. She has a long life ahead of her and allowing this tragedy to change the course of her life would be a major mistake. All of us will deal with major issues in our own lives in our own ways and it's important to understand that there is no right or wrong way to grieve. But, I do believe that it is important to control how much time you spend thinking and focusing on such a negative issue and to be cognizant of how the situation is affecting you as a person. Many times, controlling your thoughts also means being in control of who you are as a person.

Negative thoughts also can come in the form of a past event or scenario. I know a few couples, some whom are dating and some whom are married, who have dealt with issues of infidelity. In all cases, one of the members of the relationship has strayed and cheated on his or her spouse or loved one. In a few cases this has led to an end to the relationship, but in the other cases, the couples have decided to stay together to try and work through their issues and recommit themselves to one another. I know of at least two situations where the partner who was deceived cannot yet let go of the memories and feelings of being hurt and deceived. I know this is natural and I don't blame anyone for having trouble getting past the infidelity and broken trust. But eventually, the people who were hurt need to set future goals and keep themselves focused on forward progress in order to get there. Their constant focus on the negative act of their loved one would continue to cause them to feel anger and resentment towards that person—certainly preventing them from moving forward and recommitting themselves completely. With so much time, energy, and emotion spent rehashing the awful event, the deceived people are going to have an extremely difficult time ever reaching the point where they feel forgiveness. After sufficient time and discussion surrounding the event has passed, they will need to avoid dwelling on the past and focus on the present state of their relationships. For it is then that recovery, forgiveness, and forward progress can be achieved.

I've illustrated above how negative thoughts can easily be associated with past, present, or future thoughts. It's not so much where your thoughts lie that is important, but rather the nature of your thought. Are they negative or positive? Learn to identify and control your negative thoughts and you will benefit greatly, regardless if you dwell on the past, present, or future. Giving negative thoughts time, energy, and focus will only give them life in your own mind. Maintain control of your negative thinking and you will maintain control of your past memories, present day feelings, and future happiness.

(5) Be happy in SPITE of problems—things will not be perfect for life is not perfect, there is no blueprint to follow

I have been classified as a results-oriented person. Many times in my life I can recall working to accomplish something and not being satisfied or happy until it was done. My mindset in regard to anxiety was no different. While dealing with anxiety I kept thinking: *This is the only problem I have to get through, then I'll be happy.* But why couldn't I have found happiness *while* battling anxiety? After all, there were many things to be happy about during that period of my life.

I think most of us in today's society find it difficult to be happy and content when we are dealing with difficult situations in our lives. Why shouldn't you be happy today, regardless of what troubles you? Why wait, especially for things in life that may never happen? Some of us go through life thinking: *If I can just get that new job...* or *Once I make more money...* or *If I find the right person... THEN I will be happy.* Since life is full of challenges, road blocks, and downfalls, if you can find happiness in spite of having problems you will be much better off in the long run. By adapting to this way of living, you will position yourself for a much happier and more fulfilling life.

Don't wait for all to be perfect. Make yourself happy *today!* Find happiness in your mind and in your life by accepting an imperfect world—a rollercoaster ride even—and understand that things change daily. Each problem may not have an easy, tangible solution, but it will have multiple ways of being perceived. Sometimes the solution is all in the way you look at it—"solving a problem" can be as easy as altering your perception.

My graduation from Business School was held outside on a beautiful, sunny May afternoon. I don't remember the name of our commencement speaker, nor do I even remember the premise of his story, but it's funny how sometimes you hear just what you need to hear. As I swayed in and out of attentiveness, I heard the speaker say, "The more precisely you plan your future the harder destiny will hit you."

He was making reference to the fact that life is full of surprises and that there are many different roads that can be followed, all with their own experiences and endings. Obviously one can never fully plan their future, but at the time, I can remember thinking that I disagreed with this man. Up until that point in my life, I had basically planned my future successfully. I had attended the college I had planned to attend, I had chosen a career path according to my plans, and all had fallen into place. I had even lived in the cities in which I'd always dreamed of living: San Francisco, New York, and Boston. I had followed through on my plans for each of these goals. So when I tuned back into my commencement speaker and heard this statement of his, I thought that this man most likely came across a few misfortunes in his life that did not allow his plans to play out the way he had hoped. I couldn't understand how he wasn't able to follow through on what he had planned.

It wasn't until this year, almost four years later, that I finally realize what this man was talking about and now agree with him wholeheartedly. It's not about planning your weekend or where you might want to work or live. It isn't even about where you want to go to college or with whom you wanted to live. But rather, it is about being capable of rolling with the punches— the punches of life. It's about taking life as it comes and dealing with each circumstance as it arises whether planned for or not. The expected, the unexpected, the welcome and the unwelcome— these events are all minutes, hours, days, and weeks away. You can try to plan for what you know, and what you might expect to happen, but more importantly you should be prepared to "roll" with whatever comes your way.

As many of us grow up and start to manage our lives on our own, we subconsciously search for some type of plan to follow, a *blueprint* if you will. Whether we realize it or not we shape our lives around the way we were raised, our experiences and interests, and how we think about and perceive the world. Society today offers so many opportunities and technologies that there are many more roads to follow than decades ago. One might even argue that with such an incredible amount of opportunity comes greater complexity. Whether good or bad, it's this complexity that makes it much more challenging for any of us to follow any type of blueprint that we may have thought once existed.

In my own life, I grew up thinking that I would go to college, get married, have a family, and live happily ever after. Isn't that what many of us are taught to believe? Isn't that what most movies and books are based upon? As sappy as it sounds, I believed my blueprint included all of those things with certain time frames attached to each. I thought I'd be married to the love of my life by age twenty-five. Perhaps we'd have children by thirty? And I'd make a comfortable living, capable of supporting my family. An enormous house, with pristine landscaping and a white picket fence (of course) was also a part of this plan. This blueprint became embedded in my head to the point where nothing else would suffice. And when it didn't come true in the time parameters I had set for myself, my quarter-life crisis set in. I didn't realize that trying to follow a blueprint, or very specific plans, would only promote worry and anxiety if I didn't then achieve those plans.

As I've grown up, my family has seen death, divorce, and infidelity. All things I never thought I'd face in my scripted, perfect life. It wasn't until I experienced my battle with anxiety that I began to realize that life is certainly not perfect. The sooner I was able to accept and understand this, the better off I was. Life is not about the pursuit of the perfect life or the destination of one happy place. It's about enjoying the journey of an unscripted life and managing everything that comes your way. It is about living each experience as it happens and when obstacles arrive it's about learning and growing from them, and eventually, moving past them. I now live my life day by day. I make my plans for the future much broader and I don't fixate on following them exactly. I now leave room for error, change, and most importantly life, which is truly unexpected and unscripted.

I can remember thinking to myself: *Everything else in my life is great. If I can get over this anxiety, I will be happy.* Looking back it's now obvious that this was a very self-defeating thought. It's important to not only be happy when all is going well, but to learn to be happy when problems exist, *in spite* of those problems. Yes, I had an anxiety disorder. This disorder was frightening, frustrating, and demoralizing. Yet within time I found happiness in spite of that problem. It wasn't until I realized that I had to stop waiting for my anxiety disorder to go away in order to be happy that I finally turned a corner. It took time, but eventually I began to find happiness in other aspects of my life in spite of my continuous battle with severe anxiety.

(6) Be thankful for your health and the moments you are fortunate enough to live (Sonny)

Throughout this past year, at the end of a long day full of anxious episodes, worry, and panic, when all I wanted to do was give up, I would stop myself and be thankful. *I was alive.* I was physically healthy and fit and knew that I should be more appreciative of that fact. No matter how awful my anxiety disorder felt, I began to find comfort knowing that it would not truly harm me, or worse, kill me. This thought would always remind me of a friend of mine who taught me how to be truly thankful for my health. His name was Sonny.

Sonny and I first met as teammates on our college baseball team. We were very similar—both athletes, shared many of the same interests, and had personalities that just clicked (I always laughed at his jokes and he at mine). The only major difference between Sonny and I was that Sonny had Hodgkin's Disease. Hodgkin's Disease is a severe form of cancer that originates in the lymphatic tissue, which is part of your immune system. On average, roughly 1,300 Americans die each year from Hodgkin's Disease (MayoClinic.com, 2006).

Sonny had spent much of his high school and college life in and out of hospitals. Many times his condition took him away from school and our team for weeks at a time. But Sonny always came back and I so greatly admired his determination, strength, and the way he carried himself. He was never down, never upset, and always had a joke to share, even at the worst of times. He didn't sulk and feel sorry for himself. He found happiness with his family, friends, and teammates in spite of his problems because he had learned about the value of those healthy moments in his life. With a potentially fatal condition, Sonny had learned that lesson rather quickly.

In August of 1999 Sonny's condition declined dramatically. He was bedridden and restricted to spending all of his time in the hospital because the disease had progressed beyond all treatable levels. The doctors, Sonny's family, our teammates, myself, and even Sonny, knew that he wouldn't again live outside of his hospital room. I can clearly recall my car ride to see Sonny immediately after I found out that his condition had worsened. I worried about what I would say to him, what we would talk about, and how I would talk to my friend who was on his death bed. I tentatively opened his door and stepped into his room. Before I had the chance to speak, Sonny looked at me and said, "Nice hat. What, did you get a free bowl of soup with that thing?"

Using one of his favorite lines from *Caddy Shack*—one that I had heard many times before—Sonny cracked a joke and a smile! Chuckling at himself, he continued by asking me how I was doing. And he wasn't just making small talk. He was on his death bed, yet was still curious about how *I* was doing. This changed me forever.

The fact that Sonny could lie on his bed in pain, in a hospital room that he would never leave, thinking about a life that he would not live, and not only be able to crack a joke but more importantly worry about how *I* was doing has forever etched Sonny in my mind. At the time he was physically unrecognizable—bloated and hairless from the chemotherapy—yet I will always remember him as the incredibly kind, caring, and happy person that he once was. His selfless nature and the way he continued to enjoy his life in spite of his fatal disease, has had a huge impact on me. Sonny enjoyed every moment for what it was—one fortunate opportunity to live. He didn't waste precious time sulking and complaining about the horrible hand that he was dealt. He lived. And when he passed away a few short days later, I knew that I would never forget my friend Sonny, or his example about how to appreciate your health and the moments that you are fortunate enough to live.

(7) Don't be so hard on yourself

For as long as I can remember I have been my toughest critic, always hard on myself—constantly striving to achieve, succeed, and "be the best." Thankfully, for most of my life, this drive has led to many accomplishments and successes. However, this characteristic has also created unnecessary pressure and stress that have only fueled my anxiety. It made it extremely difficult for me to accept the fact that I had an anxiety disorder. This characteristic is also a likely reason why I took it so hard when I was faced with such a condition—especially one that I couldn't easily conquer or control.

If you are anything like me, you probably like to be in control. I've found that with most things in life if I work hard enough I can usually stay in control and accomplish my desired outcome. Not so with anxiety. In fact, the more I tried to control anxiety the more it actually controlled me. An important part of getting over anxiety is learning how to allow yourself to relinquish control of your feelings, your fears, and the anxiety itself. I was only able to begin to do this after I stopped being so hard on myself.

But it wasn't easy. I can remember getting so frustrated that I was dealing with an anxiety disorder that it began to make me depressed. My initial reaction to the disorder was that I was weak. At the onset of my disorder I could barely get through the most inconsequential events—a meeting at work, a dinner with my friends, sitting at home watching television. And because I constantly tried to control the disorder it became progressively worse until it reached the point where it had infiltrated every facet of my life. It affected me in the morning, the afternoon, and at night. I couldn't sleep nor could I eat. Anxiety affected everything. It became who I was, or at least who I felt I was at that time. It wasn't until I learned how to be more compassionate toward myself that I began to make forward progress with my disorder. Once I learned to accept this problem, for the time being, I was able to begin to look past the issue and focus on what to do to help myself. Rather than being so hard on myself and expending an inordinate amount of time and energy being frustrated, I began to channel that energy to start to tackle my problem directly.

This is not to say that I've change my expectations for myself, I've simply learned how to manage those expectations and treat myself with more compassion and understanding. When things go wrong, I now try to just roll with the punches and focus on the positives. This is a very important tool when dealing with anxiety. People who are very hard on themselves fuel their own anxiety. They get fed up with their anxious episodes and often get down on themselves for having allowed these episodes to continue to occur (or even occur in the first place). If you find yourself in that same mindset, take a step back and take a deep breath. Don't relate what you're experiencing to long-term problems or to who you are as a person. Know that all of these issues will one day pass and that you will be a better person for having gone through such a challenging time. Be compassionate and proud of yourself knowing that one day you will surely conquer your anxiety.

(8) Accept your feelings and don't anticipate how you will feel

Anxiety and panic attacks make your body tingle and your chest palpitate. They cause you to sweat, become dizzy, and can take your breath away. These attacks can be extremely frightening. Once you have your first anxiety or panic attack it becomes easy to understand why you would fear future attacks. For many, the slightest hint or anticipation of these symptoms can bring on the anxiety or panic attack itself. For others, the memory of an attack, coupled with one's dread and fear of another attack, will only produce more anxiety.

Learning to accept anxiety or panic symptoms and feelings rather than fear, anticipate, or fight them will help you control your anxiety. For instance, now when I walk into a meeting and feel a twinge of anxiety or shortness of breath, I accept the feelings immediately. I think to myself that it is completely natural to feel that way and I know that it doesn't mean the arrival of a full blown anxiety attack. By learning to accept my feelings (almost to the point of embracing them) my fear associated with future attacks has diminished. No longer does a "twinge" lead to the compounding of anxious feelings that would spiral out of control and develop into an anxiety or panic attack. Accepting the presence of a variety of feelings is not only an essential step in recovering from a disorder, it's a required one.

When I first began reading about anxiety I learned about the many disorders that exist (many of which I was never aware) and I was determined to diagnose my disorder. With the help of my newfound knowledge, I was able to make some predictions about my own condition. And later, with the expertise from my therapist, we confirmed some of my initial suspicions. Basically, I had developed a combination of a few of these disorders. My move back to Boston and my constant worry about where I was heading and what I wanted out of life had led to the onset of a General Anxiety Disorder. This build up of stress needed an outlet and soon caused me to have a panic attack. This attack had such a profound effect on me that I also developed a Panic Disorder. I was so shocked and surprised by my feelings of panic that I dreaded the thought of having another attack. I did not seek help immediately and as time progressed I allowed these conditions to grow and fester and I developed a moderate case of depression.

While identifying these conditions was helpful because it allowed me to learn more about them, it was also detrimental because it gave these conditions "life". It was more difficult for me to move past them because now, in my mind, they had a name! Not only was I constantly thinking and worried about the symptoms I was having but now I was worried about the actual disorder. I began to anticipate how I was going to feel each day, which of course, only added to my anxiety level. It is an evil and vicious cycle—one where fear of such attacks only fuels more anxiety which in turn usually leads to an actual attack. Dreading an attack will typically induce one.

This is similar to being diagnosed with an irregular heartbeat. Before the diagnosis, you probably didn't pay much attention to the beat of your heart so there was no worry or fear associated with it. But once you received the diagnosis, you became aware of it. You begin looking for and anticipating that irregular beat. And once you experience one, you are filled with panic and worry and begin to anticipate another. You might even mistake normal heartbeats for irregular beats simply because you are focused on monitoring it. Many times, looking for symptoms can actually produce them. This is very similar to what I experienced. I began to constantly monitor the way I felt. I'd look for anxious symptoms and, in reality, I was creating them.

This also reminds me of a friend, Lauren, who lost her best friend, Sarah, to a brain aneurism. One second Sarah was fine, and the next, she fell to the ground and passed away. Her brain had hemorrhaged causing her to die instantaneously. Lauren spent the next year fearing this fate for herself. She was convinced that she was destined for the same fate, and so she didn't sleep or eat normally for months. She too developed an anxiety disorder based on her fear of dying. Because Lauren was extremely focused on brain aneurisms, and even anticipated experiencing one herself, anytime she felt uneasy or had a headache she actually thought she might die. Her awareness and knowledge was creating her anxiety.

Unfortunately, these worries are natural. Our knowledge can often times be detrimental to our happiness. I now understand the saying, *ignorance is bliss*. But make no mistake, it *is* important to be educated. The goal, though, is to educate yourself while simultaneously not fearing what may or may not happen to you. Anticipating your irregular heartbeat will only produce worry.

Anticipating that you may have a brain aneurism and die instantly will surely take away the enjoyment of living. Likewise, anticipating that you might feel anxious or panic in a particular situation will only validate this concern and allow your anxiety to build.

(9) Put it into perspective—don't let anxiety become your main focus

In my experience, people similar to me who are motivated, results-oriented, and accustomed to identifying and solving problems quickly, tend to be compulsive about problems until they are amended. And with anxiety, it is no different. People with this type of personality have what can be referred to as an "always/everything" personality trait. This term refers to the way certain people process the thoughts and events that occur in their lives, along with how they perceive their problems. If you view problems as *always* and *everything*, you typically feel the problem will *always* exist and that it will affect *everything* in your life. People who view the world with an *always/everything* personality are much more susceptible to developing an anxiety disorder.

So, how do we try to alter this personality trait and become a *not always / not everything* type of person? We do so by trying not to let our problems become our main, and only, focus. Also, by learning to put your problems into perspective many times it can help you minimize their effect on you and allow you to focus on other things in your life.

There is one simple phrase that I say to myself often that helps me out tremendously—*put it on the backburner*. When I first began developing issues with anxiety I typically only thought about anxiety when I was at work because that was where it originated. But as my battle with anxiety progressed and developed into a full blown anxiety disorder, it became all that I thought about. I woke up fearing it, went through my day worrying about it, and went to bed thinking about it. My anxiety disorder ruled my life. It wasn't until I was able to *put it on the backburner* that I began to gain control over it. My anxiety didn't go away immediately but the better I became at preventing myself from focusing on it and allowing myself to think about other aspects of my life, the sooner I began to overcome my disorder.

In fact, I can remember a day last August. It was a gorgeous summer day and I was on vacation in Nantucket. A few days into the trip, I found myself sitting at dinner with a bunch of friends. In between conversations it hit me that I hadn't been anxious at dinner that night. I hadn't been shaking my legs under the table, wanting to leave, or compulsively thinking about my disorder. I was actually focused on my friends' conversations. In fact, it hit me that I hadn't been thinking about my disorder much that entire day. It was the first day that I could say this. Prior to that, I went through most days completely preoccupied with thoughts of my anxiety disorder, allowing those thoughts to make me angry and upset.

Placing your issues and problems on the backburner is a must as is putting them into perspective. The first few months of my anxiety disorder were terrible. I didn't think I'd ever get past my feelings. I thought that I'd go through the rest of my life anxious, depressed, and hindered. But over time I was able to put my disorder into perspective. I wasn't dying, nor could my anxiety kill me. I was leading a very fortunate life with great friends, a good job, a prospering career, and many other blessings. I was letting this one issue, my anxiety disorder, negate all of the positives in my life. I wasn't putting things into perspective. It took quite a while before I realized that my problems could have been much worse.

My therapist, Janet Fronk, would always say, "This too shall pass." I think it's a great way for you to view your problems. Unless it is life threatening, within time those problems too shall pass. It may not seem like it while you are struggling with your problems—particularly an anxiety disorder or depression which can make you feel hopeless—but eventually, the problems will pass. If you have faith in this statement and remember it in times of difficulty, I'm confident that it will help give you a different outlook on your problems. Remember, *this too shall pass.*

(10) Have courage—bring it on!

If you're in the midst of an anxiety disorder and have yet to turn the corner, you are probably more concerned about how you can fight this anxiety today. Rather than look at your anxiety as a problem or a disorder, take a different perspective and look at it as a challenge—your challenge! It is what you need to fight today and it takes a great deal of patience, perseverance, and courage to do so.

There are a great deal of people in this world who have to fight cancer, physical handicaps, and many other major challenges. Anxiety is your challenge. It may not seem fair in your eyes, and perhaps it's not, but it is a reality. The sooner you accept this, the sooner you will be on your way to conquering it. You can either wake up each morning fearing the day and being afraid and tentative or you can wake up and acknowledge that you need to be courageous and prepare for battle that day. Rather than shy away from fighting your anxiety, adapt a new attitude—*bring it on!* Conquering it is possible.

(11) **Be happy with progress and know that this will pass**

There is no quick fix to getting over an anxiety disorder. It takes time. When I first experienced severe anxiety, I kept wishing I'd wake up the next day and it would all be forgotten, as if it had been a bad dream. I'd set time parameters for when I hoped to be back to "normal" and when I didn't achieve them, I would get angry and upset with myself. I'd then set new parameters and when those days came and went, I'd continue to feel defeated. It became a vicious cycle.

After some time I finally realized that it's important to be happy with the *slightest* bit of progress along the way. Chances are you aren't going to wake up one day and suddenly be fully recovered. You will most likely have to put in a great deal of time and effort and will experience an up and down recovery path before you get better. It wasn't until I acknowledged this and formed a new long term plan—one that did not include an exact recovery deadline or a specific thought about how I should feel in a finite amount of time—that I began to make progress. More importantly, I became happy with *any* progress that I made, large or small.

It is also important to understand that you will have good and bad days. When dealing with an anxiety disorder it's only natural that after a bad day you wonder, *is it back?!* After I had turned the corner with my own disorder, I'd have one or two weeks of good progress followed immediately by a bad day (or two). When this happened I'd immediately think that I was falling back into the anxiety driven lows that I'd once experienced. These up and down cycles continued for months until I finally learned to identify the bad days as just that—bad days. Then, I began to make consistent progress. One bad day would no longer dictate how I thought I would feel the next day, or the day after that. When I finally realized that bad days are independent of my disorder and the previous day, I began to find happiness in my progress.

(12) Better for going through this
I can remember wishing that this anxiety disorder had never happened to me and that I

would just be "normal" again. In fact, for months, my goal was to get back to being normal—and in my eyes being normal meant being the person I was before my anxiety disorder ever developed. It meant being happy, having fun, having a very positive outlook on life and being capable of doing anything I wanted without panic or worry—basically it meant being anxiety-free. But after recovering from my anxiety disorder I never did return to the same person I once was. In fact, I never got the same life back that I once had. I found a *better* place in life and I became a *better* person. I am now more knowledgeable about myself and the way I think and perceive the world. I am much more educated about anxiety and I've obtained the skills needed to combat it. This has made me stronger. Today I am a stronger man. My experiences will provide me with a lifetime of knowledge and protection so that anxiety will never again sneak up on me.

My experience with anxiety has also made me a much more grateful person. I look back on my tough experiences as motivation and reason to appreciate my life today. Whether this happened to me when it did or years down the road, it was bound to happen. Being unaware of the thinking patterns, symptoms, and personality traits that provoke anxiety would surely have hurt me at some point in my life. I view the fact that I dealt with this issue when I did as a blessing. The fact that I've learned how to overcome and prevail against anxiety will only strengthen me for years to come. To put it bluntly, I am much better for going through this.

I think it's a natural reaction for your mind to wish you were that same person prior to your attack or disorder. Your mind is looking for a peaceful time and place when you didn't have the burden of anxiety every second of every day. It's looking for security. It thinks back to a time when anxiety was not an issue and views that time as burden free. But why wish for that? Why wish for mediocrity when you are on the verge of greatness? An anxiety disorder can change your life forever—for the good or for the bad—it's up to you.

You can forever wish away your disorder along with all of the negative experiences and knowledge that you've derived from it. Or you can turn this struggle into a positive. You can view everything you went through as a learning experience. Once you do this you will understand all that anxiety encompasses and from that knowledge you will grow. Your personal growth is the armor you will use in the future to fight anxiety before it ever again becomes a disorder. It will provide you with confidence, knowledge, and a sense of achievement for defeating this mighty adversary.

(13) Maximize the positives—turn negatives into positives

This strategy doesn't only apply to anxiety but to life in general. For most of us we have the innate ability to easily focus on the negatives in our lives rather than the positives. When walking down the street do you think about how lucky you are to be healthy and alive? Or do you walk down the street complaining to yourself about your sore legs, family spat, irate boss, or work stress? Most likely it's the latter. How about when waking up in the morning? Do you think, *Oh I wish I didn't have to go to work today?* Or do you think, *Wow, I am lucky to have a job and can't wait to go!* Most likely it's the former, and unfortunately, this manner of thinking appears to be human nature which makes it difficult to stray from. But there is a happy medium. By making ourselves aware of this tendency, we can control our negative thoughts and potentially turn them into positives!

Think for a moment that it's an early Monday morning in late February. It's cold and dark outside. Your alarm clock goes off at six a.m. It's time to get up and get ready for work. You would love to sleep a few more hours but you know you can't, an important eight o'clock meeting is on your calendar. In fact, you are the host of the meeting and your boss will be looking for answers from you on a particular project in which he recently put you in charge. You rush to get ready for work, scoff down a quick bowl of cereal, and run out the door. Sitting behind the wheel of your fairly new car, you turn the key in the ignition, and of course, it won't start! A sixty-dollar cab ride later and you arrive at work with only ten minutes to setup for your presentation. How would you interpret that morning? I bet most people would be angry, stressed, and irritated, perhaps cursing the whole morning while rushing around allowing their anxiety to grow. A few years ago I probably would have as well.

Now, I am not saying you shouldn't be upset if you were involved in the above scenario. I think any normal human being would. But you have a choice in how you can interpret these occurrences. I would suggest taking a step back and trying to view all that happened in a different light, with a different point of view. Read the short scenario again. Try to pick out a few positives. Can you? Rather than dread going into work that day perhaps you could be thankful that you have a job to go to and consider yourself fortunate. Not only do you have a job, it appears you have a job where your superior respects your skills and opinion enough to put you in charge of a very important project. Also, what about the car not starting? Obviously that would get all of us rattled and angry. I too expect things to work when they should. But perhaps you could find happiness in the fact that you have a car. Or better yet, that you have a new car! That's surely a nice luxury. Lastly, I'm sure most of us would hate to spend sixty dollars of our own money on a cab to take us to work because our car didn't start. That's a fair assessment. But, why focus on wasting sixty bucks when you can rest happily at night knowing you have a job and a future income source?

After a morning like that I don't expect anyone to whistle his or her way into the office. For most of us it would be almost impossible to focus on only the positive aspects of that morning. It's alright to get angry, but when your anger has subsided it's important not to harp on the negatives. Instead, reevaluate the scenario and focus on the positives, or even better, try to move on and not fixate on the details of that morning at all. As irritating as it might have been, you did arrive at work on time. So once there, you really didn't need to harp on the dreadful events that led you there that morning. Bring your mind to the present moment and focus on the positives regardless of how you got there. Being present and maximizing the positives can be like starting your day over.

Someone once told me that the key to life is to turn everything into a positive. I can remember hearing this and immediately thinking it was impossible. How can a person turn *everything* into a positive? Life is full of so many negative events that there is no way one can view them all in a positive light. It wasn't until my battle with my anxiety that I learned that this is, in fact, possible and attainable. A few words of caution though—if you try to turn a negative into a positive immediately after it happens, you might have trouble doing so. It's usually takes time in order to look at the situation objectively and spin it into a positive experience.

As I was battling my anxiety disorder I never thought I'd be able to view it in a positive light. But after time passed I realized what a valuable, positive experience it was for me go through. Actually, in many ways I am thankful for it because it helped me become a better person. It gave me knowledge, strength, and the know-how to overcome future fear or worry. It has also given me a much better understanding of myself, my goals, and what I want out of my future. However, I know that I wouldn't have viewed it as favorably six months ago, so just remember that it takes time and effort to turn negatives into positives.

A great example of this is the story of my athletic career. A baseball player since the age of five, I basically grew up in the front yard of my neighbor's house hitting wiffle balls all day long, pretending to be Jose Canseco or Mark McGwire. I continued playing through elementary, junior high, and high school and was fortunate to receive a scholarship to play baseball in college. I had a nice college career, set a few records, and tweaked the interest of a few professional scouts. As time passed it became clear that playing baseball was not just a love but a career goal in my life. At age twenty-one I was chasing my lifelong dream to become a professional baseball player and I actually had a shot. But with two weeks left of my senior season a severe back and neck injury abruptly ended my career . . . and my dream. Contact from baseball scouts basically ceased and the Major League Baseball Draft came and went rather quickly. I didn't get drafted and this was a tough blow. My lifelong dream had ended—in failure.

Two weeks later I went to work for the Fortune 500 Company that I still work for today. I was quite lucky to have a great job lined up as my "Plan B", never thinking that this plan would become my only option. I spent the next few years working hard and climbed from one position to another. Today I am grateful for the opportunities I've received and the career I've enjoyed thus far. I realize that I would never have had this opportunity or be where I am today had I continued to play baseball.

For years though I viewed my absence from the world of baseball as a personal failure. It affected me quite deeply for a long time and I had a difficulty accepting the fact that I never made it. After many years I was able to look back and view the end of my baseball career as a blessing. If I were drafted I would have surely went and played minor league baseball for a few years, leaving my business opportunities behind. Being honest with myself now, I know I could have played in the minors for a few years but would never have made it to the Major Leagues (I was good, but not *that* good). If I pursued baseball, I would have started my business career three to five years later and probably would have never had time to go back and get my MBA. I would have been years behind where I am today. After years had gone by I finally was able to look back at my disappointment, the biggest one of my life, and turn it into a positive. I never would be where I am today if my life had followed a different path and today I am grateful for that.

As my life rolls on I now find myself looking for the good in every situation, especially the very bad ones. And to my surprise, I have found success in doing this. As I mentioned earlier, six months ago I would have said that my battle with anxiety would never be classified as a positive experience. Today, I stand corrected. Just like my baseball career, my struggle with anxiety has been turned into a positive. Not only do I view myself as a stronger and better person but my battle also prompted the writing of this book, which will hopefully help many of you.

(14) Anxiety will become less captive and scary

When I first developed my anxiety disorder I didn't know anything about the condition or what it truly entailed. I didn't know that the disorder would distort my thoughts, my feelings, and my perception of life. I didn't realize the impact it would have on me. All I knew was that suddenly I was hesitant to do many of the things I once did without anxiety or worry.

As I struggled daily with my anxiety disorder, I yearned for the day I would be recovered. I thought the only way I'd be happy was if I was fully recovered from the captive feelings and symptoms my anxiety disorder bestowed upon me. But what I've learned is totally different from what I had initially hoped for. I've learned that it wasn't that my anxiety needed to go away in order for me to move forward but rather that my ability to manage it needed to grow stronger and become more capable. It wasn't that I needed to stop feeling anxious but rather that my perception and fear of my anxiety needed to change.

What I've learned is now clear in my mind— I will always be an anxious person for I will always strive to be the best that I can be. Life will certainly produce stress and I will continue to put myself in anxious situations as I try to grow and better myself in this world. My anxiety will never completely disappear (after all it is a natural part of human nature) but I will be able to better control and manage it. My awareness and knowledge of anxiety will alleviate any and all of the scary and captive feelings that it once had over me. My experiences have given me the ability to keep my anxiety where it should be—healthy, motivating, and useful.

(15) **<u>Be comfortable with yourself wherever you are</u>**

Once you've experienced an anxiety or panic attack you will most likely begin to fear having another one. This fear can build as your mind searches for ways around these attacks such as avoiding certain places or events. Unfortunately, many people even succumb to the fear by becoming less social. I've learned about people who no longer leave their house once they develop an anxiety disorder. I can now relate to them and understand how they feel. Their disorder is called *agoraphobia* and it's a fear of open or public places. For those people their home is viewed as their domain—the only place where they feel safe— hence why they shy away from leaving it. They don't fear attacks in their safe domain.

Because my initial anxiety attack occurred in a conference room at work, I feared going into a meeting in a conference room for months afterward. I worried that I would have an attack and one of my colleague's would notice. I feared embarrassing myself or having my colleagues think I was less capable of handling my job. This fear slowly grew into a discomfort that happened in any situation where I felt trapped. Because of this, I couldn't even sit through a meal with friends or attend church with my family without focusing on my anxious feelings and fearing the worst.

During my struggle with anxiety, I attended a wedding of one of my best friends. Even before the day of the wedding, I wondered if I would be able to sit through the church and enjoy myself. The day of the wedding soon came and as I entered the church I contemplated sitting towards the back in case I needed to leave. I then remembered the promise I had made to myself earlier in my struggle to never let this disorder dictate my decisions, so I made my way towards the front of the church and found a seat. It wasn't more than a few minutes into the wedding when I began to feel my anxiety grow. I couldn't take control of my thoughts and worried about how awful it would be to have an attack right there. I soon began sweating and my heart pounded hard and fast. My anxious feelings compounded upon one another and, like before, I had an overwhelming urge to just get out of that church!

But I didn't leave. One thing I learned from the very beginning is that no matter how awful my anxious feelings are or become, they won't kill me. So I fought to change my mind and focus on something that was going on around me. I looked at my friend and his soon-to-be wife. I looked around the church. I began reading the ceremony agenda. My body slowly lost that urge to run out of the church. I continued to focus on other thoughts rather my anxiety and soon the attack began to pass.

It was that experience, and others like it, that taught me that I didn't need to be home or in a safe place to feel comfortable. Being comfortable is a state of mind. It is taking control of your thoughts and feelings and determining how you feel rather than letting your thoughts determine how you feel. As I mentioned earlier, an anxiety disorder can make many people feel that they can only be safe in their homes or when they are alone. It makes them shy away from social events and typically hinders outgoing personalities. This tendency is a natural feeling with an anxiety disorder but it's imperative to fight through this. If this sounds like what you are going through, taking yourself out of society or any environment is the wrong answer. You cannot conquer anxiety by running or hiding. When you are ready, you need to fight it head on and put yourself back into the situations where you previously felt anxious or scared. You can only learn to control your anxiety by participating in life. As much as your mind and body may be telling you that you need to be in a safe place in order to feel comfortable, do not yield to this belief. You have the ability to find comfort and security in any situation. It's all a matter of how you manage your thoughts, not how they manage you.

Conquering anxiety is finding comfort within yourself no matter where you are. Janet Fronk told me the way to do this is to polish and perfect the six C's:

1) **C**ontrol thoughts
2) **C**hallenge what life brings
3) **C**ommitment to success
4) **C**loseness of relationships
5) **C**ourage to face life's obstacles
6) **C**onfidence in the outcome

Mastering these skills (or at least strengthening them) will allow you security and peace within yourself. Whether you are in a meeting, an airplane, a church, or even a very small enclosed area, being comfortable is in *your mind.* The sooner you can find your internal comfort and security, the sooner you will be able to apply them to your daily life and realize comfort is in your mind regardless of where your physical body may reside.

These fifteen points that I've carried with me in my wallet for the past year have truly changed my life. They are the skills that helped me recover from an anxiety disorder and are reminders of all that I've learned. They are a mixture of my own research, my experiences, and instruction from my sessions with Janet Fronk. They are all statements that have truly resonated with me and they all represent a lesson I've learned about my own life. Hopefully you can derive similar effects from some, if not all, of these points.

11

Recovery: Time, Commitment, Faith—and Breathing

Recovery takes time, commitment, and faith. It takes time and commitment to learn how to practice the skills needed to combat anxiety so that they one day become second nature to you. It also takes time for the awful feelings that accompany an anxiety disorder to become a distant memory. Similar to a tough breakup, initially it hurts and it is all you can think about. You think that you'll never be happy again or that you'll never get over the pain. But eventually you do and that is where faith comes in. It takes faith to get through those anxious times in your life and believe that one day things will improve, for eventually they do.

Having faith is one of the most important elements in conquering an anxiety disorder, or even depression. Faith that these feelings are

- 159 -

temporary and that they will eventually pass. It's important to realize that you *will* get over an anxiety disorder and recover. During the first few months of my disorder, I did not have any faith that I'd ever get over my anxiety disorder. Without faith, I had no hope and a very dismal outlook on my future. It wasn't until I began to have faith in my recovery due to my therapy, research, and numerous conversations with friends and family, that I began to feel better. Developing faith gave me hope, and hope was what I needed to recover.

Having faith can also mean something more. For some, it can have religious overtones. I am a practicing Catholic. I am not extremely active in my church but I do pray and try to lead a life based on the beliefs and rules laid forward by the Catholic church. I do not attend mass regularly, nor do I adhere to every Catholic principle outlined in the Bible, but I do believe in God and do appreciate the life that I have been given. That being said, I can remember Janet Fronk asking me about my religion. I wondered why she wanted to know as I didn't think anxiety and religion had any correlation. When I told her that I was

Catholic she told me that looking to God to guide me through this difficult time could be part of my recovery. She left it up to me but explained that many people pray for various things, including an anxiety-free life. In fact, it is so prevalent that many Catholic priests include a reference to it in their weekly masses. Janet said that the next time I was in church I should listen to the prayer that the priest recites just before passing out the communion. This prayer asks for guidance and strength from God against a number of evil things, including anxiety. Sure enough she was right. The next time I went to church I heard the priest ask God to "keep us free from anxiety."

Wow, if Catholic priests ask God to keep us all free from anxiety it must be a much more prevalent problem than I first anticipated. It couldn't be any more clear that anxiety has plagued people for generations. This justification provided me with an overwhelming sense of normalcy and strengthened both my participation in my religion and my faith in my recovery. I knew I would eventually get through my battle with anxiety.

Having faith that you will overcome your disorder is crucial. When I met up with my good friend, Lane, that beautiful Sunday afternoon in New York, we talked about her anxiety. She, like me initially, did not know much about anxiety or how to go about fighting it. She had yet to invest the time and commitment needed to learn about and attack her disorder. Also, she had yet to develop the faith that she would eventually overcome the effects and symptoms that had begun to control her days and nights. She did not believe she would get past her condition.

In the first ten minutes of our conversation it was obvious that Lane had many of the same thoughts and symptoms that I once had. For example, most of Lane's anxiety was coming from her habit of future thinking. I explained to her my interpretation of mindfulness and how to focus on your breathing rather than future thoughts. Instead of worrying about whether you will be married in five years or if you will be happy, simply focus on your breathing instead for a few seconds, minutes, or even longer. It's a great interruption for a person who finds themselves constantly focused on the future, especially potentially harmful future thoughts. I think it was the first time Lane realized that her thoughts were driving her anxiety. It was also the first time she acknowledged the need to spend the time to practice such a technique, and commit herself to getting better.

To better illustrate the importance of breathing I asked Lane to identify the first thing she did whenever she got nervous, anxious, or scared. She thought about it and really couldn't answer. She acted out how she would react if she were scared or nervous and still couldn't answer the question. But as an onlooker, I could answer for her. Like most people Lane held her breath. Most of us do this when we are startled or shocked. It's an innate reaction. Our body tenses up and we momentarily hold our breath. This only heightens our anxiety and the lack of oxygen can actually cause a panic attack.

It's important to understand that without your mind your body is not an intelligent, functioning being. Your body alone cannot determine right from wrong or thought from reality. It relies on the mind to send communication that will dictate how it should react and then responds accordingly. Constant worry and anxiety puts your body on alert and when your mind signals that there is something wrong, your body reacts defensively. Holding your breath sends a signal to your body that all is not well. Fearing a problem, your body produces more anxiety and your fight or flight response kicks in. When there's no ensuing fight or flight your body then begins searching for a release to this anxiety overload. It looks for an outlet. Quite often this outlet is an anxiety or panic attack.

While speaking with Lane I remembered my first visit with Janet Fronk. She took a strawberry lifesaver out of her pocket. She handed it to me and asked me to unwrap it. I did so. She then asked that I put it under my nose and close to my mouth. "Smell it," she said. I did and we continued to look at each other. She didn't say anything right away but then asked if I noticed anything. I told her "no".

"Did your mouth water?" she asked. I thought about it and yes, in fact, it had watered. She explained to me that when I smelled the strawberry lifesaver my mind registered the candy as an edible treat. It then sent signals to my mouth that I was about to eat it. I never anticipated eating the lifesaver, nor did I even allow my mouth to taste it, but my mouth watered because my mind told me I would soon be tasting it. This was a very valuable and powerful lesson and Lane agreed. If the mind thinks something is happening or about to happen, like eating this candy, the body will react, regardless if the event actually happens or not.

Lane thought about this example for a moment and asked me a question, "Knowing what you just explained, if you control your thoughts and ultimately your mind, then you should be able to control your whole body and the way you feel, right?"

I chuckled but agreed, "Yes, but that's easier said than done." Although I don't know anyone who has complete control over his or her mind and/or body, I do believe it is feasible to an extent. With time, commitment, faith, and breathing, you can improve the control you have over your mind, and ultimately your body and feelings. The goal should be to strengthen our internal thought process as well as improving the level of control that we possess over our thoughts. I am a firm believer in the great benefits even just partial control can have on our health and our psyche. Having control over your thoughts is not only healthy, it's empowering!

12

When Anxiety Leads to Depression

Most times anxiety and depression coexist. 80% of the time a person who experiences one also experiences the other (www.zoloft.com). Whether anxiety leads to depression or depression leads to anxiety is not the major issue. The major issue is that the combination of the two conditions can be quite debilitating. The chemical imbalance in your brain that has been proven to cause and aid anxiety is very similar to the shift and imbalance that accompanies depression. That is why anti-anxiety medications (SSRIs) are also anti-depression medications, for they treat anxiety and depression simultaneously. They can do this because the two are so similar in genetic structure.

As I researched more about anxiety and depression I began to wonder if I was originally depressed. I wondered what came first, my anxiety or my depression. I worried that I might have been subconsciously depressed which may have ultimately led to my anxiety. I read about people who were chronically or genetically depressed. Many times they never even knew they were depressed until years later. I started to get nervous that I had something wrong deep inside of me that wasn't just anxiety. Early on I can remember asking a good friend, who has known me for ten years, if I had ever seemed depressed to him. He laughed and replied, "You? God no. I know people who are clinically depressed and who have had life-long battles with depression—my sister for one—and you are by far not one of them. I would never have thought of you as even being remotely close to depressed."

It was good to hear his external opinion and substantiate my own curious thoughts as to whether my disorder originated as depression or anxiety. Whether it's the negative societal stigma or just my own opinion I felt better admitting that I had anxiety rather than depression. But I was not completely satisfied. Regardless of which came first it didn't matter, I was depressed now! My future looked grim. But rightfully so, what fun is it to live with an anxiety disorder? The longer you allow this anxiety to rule your life the more susceptible you are to depression. When an anxiety disorder becomes a part of your life it can take away all hope. This loss of hope obviously has an effect on your psyche and if not treated, depression is sure to follow.

In the thick of my anxiety disorder I remember thinking to myself, *what is there to look forward to or be happy about?* I can remember seeing my parents one weekend and I looked at my father and wondered how he felt inside. Was he happy? What made him tick? I looked at him and asked him, "Dad, what makes you happy? I mean, maybe not just now, but over the course of your life. I'm not seeing anything in my future that is going to make me happy." He looked at me a bit puzzled but understood what I was going through in regard to my recent struggle with anxiety. He began to think and listed a bunch of great moments he enjoyed in his life. Moments I should look forward to. "Buying a new home, starting a new job, meeting somebody new, getting married, having children, getting a promotion, or even buying a new car. These are all events that you will one day enjoy. But more importantly, just enjoy yourself and your life. Enjoy each day. There doesn't have to be a major event for you to be happy. You have to learn to be happy with just yourself, and perhaps your family and your health." That was great advice. In fact, it's advice that I still take to heart today.

I knew what my father was talking about but at the time I wasn't in the right frame of mind to comprehend what he meant. The thought of those things did not make me happy at that time. Rather than look forward to the event of buying a new car, I allowed my mind to look past that moment and see myself in that new car months later after the excitement had worn off. In my mind, once the initial joy of that exciting purchase had worn off I would resume my battle with anxiety. My anxiety was so entrenched in my everyday life that I allowed its negative impact to overshadow my joy and happiness. No matter how great a moment, my anxiety would always be there waiting for me. This thought continuously made me depressed.

When I thought about meeting somebody for the first time or getting married, I again allowed my mind to move past the original excitement and focus on the negative aspects of a relationship—issues that can develop as time passes. What if I get married and get bored with my wife? What if she gets bored with me? What if I fall out of love with her? Or get divorced? All of these thoughts were running through my mind and taking away any thoughts of excitement that would surely accompany meeting a great person. Essentially, I was allowing my anxiety disorder to overshadow all of the enjoyable events that would one day grace my life. Rather than see the positive aspects in each, I found myself fast forwarding through those moments and focusing on the less enjoyable aspects that I thought would quickly follow.

Just like anything in life, you can look at any given situation in many different ways. If you focus on the negative aspects and overlook the positives of course your outlook on life is going to be dim. An anxiety disorder and depression tend to sway your thoughts toward the more negative ones. Today I look forward to many of the same events that once seemed bleak. They no longer seem trite or unappealing to me. I look at the things my father mentioned and I look forward to each and every one of them and hundreds more. And most importantly, like he said, I simply look forward to each day and enjoy my life for what it is. My life is no longer controlled nor haunted by anxiety or depression. My future outlook is much more appealing now that I am in control of my thoughts and my anxiety. Each day is something I look forward to and what I learned most is that it all came from within. It's not that any of the events that once seemed so grim have changed; it's simply the way that I view and perceive them now that has changed.

I've also encountered people who had developed depression first yet experience anxiety as well. For people who are used to living happy and fulfilling lives, it can be a very anxious time for them to find themselves in a depressed state. Especially if this depression develops unexpectedly and one day blindsides an individual with all of the negative symptoms that accompany such a disorder. Anxiety is often present when we don't like how things are going and foresee the issue continuing into our future.

In my opinion, it really doesn't matter which came first or which caused which—anxiety or depression. For these two disorders are so similar in symptoms, causes, and recovery that they both can be treated simultaneously. But what is important to know is that they often coexist, so don't be alarmed by their combined presence. Depression is often linked to suicide so it becomes a scary thought when you realize you may be depressed. Don't be. Suicide is never the answer nor do I believe it is the sole result of a disorder. Suicide is the easy way out. It's a decision, a decision typically made by people who don't have the faith, courage, and hope to battle their problems. They don't think they can ever win so they give up. If you don't give up you will never have to worry about suicide, so don't fear it.

Whether anxiety leads to depression or depression to anxiety, rest assured that recovery is an option. You can and will recover. Accept each for what they are, disorders at a point of time in your life. It is normal and natural for such disorders to coexist. Many times I found myself trying to distinguish which was worse or which was which. I can remember many days feeling like I was more anxious than depressed and other days feeling more depressed than anxious. But soon I accepted these feelings as temporary and let them run their course, regardless of which one was more prevalent that day. Whether I was anxious or depressed for a given day didn't matter, my faith and determination eventually outweighed each of these feelings and I began feeling better.

13

Not Just Another Statistic

Throughout this book I introduced you to a few good friends of mine who have had their own issues with anxiety. Their shared stories, experiences, and struggles were a tremendous help in my battle. Their experiences gave me a sense of comfort because they helped me feel that I wasn't alone. Also, listening to accounts from people who I knew well, trusted, and respected made it clear that I wasn't *just another statistic.* Their anxiety attacks, panic attacks, lack of sleep, loss of appetite, and bouts with depression reassured me that my experiences were of the norm for someone in the midst of an anxiety disorder. But most importantly, their stories gave me the hope that one day I too would overcome my disorder.

The remarkable part about learning about these experiences was that many of these people were close friends yet I had never known anything about their struggles. Their stories helped me the most—more than reading any anxiety research publications or any of the books written by professionals. Yet if I hadn't broached the subject with my friends I would never have heard their accounts. This certainly drove home the point that discussion about anxiety is not commonplace within my group of friends, never mind in most places around the country. If it was, I would have known more about anxiety at its onset and could have battled it sooner and more effectively.

I attribute much of my recovery to my friends and their willingness to share their stories with me. It's amazing that of my close friends, 90% had experienced similar struggles with anxiety. And the few who had not, had at least one or two other friends who had. So for those of you who do not feel comfortable sharing your problems and feelings with your family or friends, or for those of you who feel alone, scared, and secluded in the midst of an anxiety disorder, I hope you can read about my experiences (and those of my friends) and feel a bit more comforted. At the very least, you will learn about others' anxiety struggles and some ways you might be able to protect yourself if you are ever faced with an anxiety battle.

Many people don't have someone close in their lives with whom they can share their innermost thoughts and feelings. A recent study revealed that 25% of America has no one to confide in (*American Sociological Review, June 22nd, 2006*). If you are someone who feels you don't have another person to share your experiences with, or maybe you just aren't much for talking about your personal feelings, then these stories are especially for you.

Towards the end of college my friend, Jeff, began having panic and anxiety attacks that drove him into a moderate depression. He had trouble sitting through his classes and started to dislike public places. He too was surprised by his anxiety disorder and was caught off guard by all of its symptoms. He admitted to me that his lack of knowledge in regard to anxiety drove him deeper into his depression. In Jeff's case, his anxiety was driven by soon-to-be changes in his life. An injury halted Jeff's athletic career a few months prior to graduation and all of a sudden he was no longer an athlete with a potential athletic future. He had to adapt to a new life and become a new person very quickly. In fact, he had three months to find a job and a career that interested him. The pressure Jeff put on himself to become this different person only promoted more stress and anxiety. It was very difficult for Jeff to let go of the person he had been for so long. For fifteen years, he had viewed himself as an athlete and the day after his injury he was no longer that person. He didn't realize this transition from athlete to non-athlete would be so tough. More importantly, he did not know that he was causing anxiety to build up inside of him until one day he had his first panic attack and, like me, his life was changed forever.

I also introduced you to Lane, one of the major reasons I wrote this book. Her quarter-life crisis crept up on her in the form of stress that she put on herself to figure out what she wanted to do with her life. Lane is a few years shy of thirty and she works and lives in New York City. Her dream is to be an actress and travel the world, yet she's stuck in a public relations career and tied to her life in New York. She lacks passion for her career and the purpose that some people have for what they do. Lane had also been monitoring her transition from young girl to responsible woman and wondering whether getting married and having children were in her future. This worry prompted Lane's anxiety and she began to lose her appetite, lie awake at night, and gradually lose interest in all of the things that she once enjoyed.

The day I spent with Lane in New York City changed both of our lives. For me, it was the spark I needed to write this book. For Lane, it was the day she realized that her over thinking had been the culprit for her anxiety and decided to speak to a professional therapist. Today, Lane is doing extremely well. She has yet to figure out what she wants to do with her life but has come to terms with the fact that that is alright—she doesn't need to know just yet. She enjoys New York City, her friends, and a new job. Her new job is not necessarily her dream job, but now she takes things day by day and worries less about whether or not she'll be happy doing it for the rest of her life. She has also learned that her over thinking was driving her anxiety. She now controls her thoughts and her mind and finds empowerment in that.

When I introduced you to Shane I told you that he was very similar to me, but four years older. Shane had stumbled upon his quarter-life crisis at about the same age that I did. Like me, he was surprised and shocked by what he experienced each day. Anxiety caught him off guard as well. Shane never had to deal with actual panic attacks, but rather developed constant and general anxiety. He didn't sleep well, couldn't eat, had severe shortness of breath (mostly when he worked out) and many times dealt with abnormal heart palpitations. Soon Shane began to give up doing things in his life that he once enjoyed. He stopped jogging, going to the gym, and going out at night. His anxiety disorder became so potent and frustrating that it drove him into depression. He began to lie in bed until noon and showed up late for work on many occasions. He just didn't want to get out of bed anymore. His job, career, and social life struggled.

Shane finally sought help after a few months. Like me he tried to battle this disorder on his own, but to no avail. He agreed that the biggest step he took was admitting to himself that he had a problem and that he needed help. Shane hit a point in his life where his career and job were stale and turning thirty and still being single began to worry him. He compounded his stress and worry by constantly trying to answer the question that many people struggle with: *What do I want to do with my life?*

In the midst of his anxiety and depression, Shane became a Big Brother to a young boy who did not have much. He didn't have a family and lived in a foster home. Shane found time each week to take this boy out to lunch, baseball games, and to the movies. Obviously, this benefited the young boy as it gave him someone to look up to and learn from. It also benefited Shane at a time when he needed it most. It put meaning and purpose back into his life and gave him a reason to get out of bed each morning. Today, four years later, Shane still faithfully picks up his Little Brother each week. Their relationship has flourished and they've both had an enormous impact on one another. Shane is happy again and enjoying other aspects of his life—he goes on vacation, works out daily, and sees his friends socially. He has also changed jobs and his way of thinking, and has grown from his experience with anxiety and depression. Like me, he now tries to live day-to-day and enjoy what he has in front of him rather than worry about what the future may or may not bring.

If you remember Bridget then you'd know that she appeared to have everything—a loving husband, a happy marriage, a wonderful home, financial stability, and a healthy baby boy. She looks happy on the outside yet still struggles internally with anxiety and depression, stemming from what I classify as having *arrived*. She has accomplished all that she set out to do, yet she is still very unhappy and anxious—most likely because she doesn't know what to do next. She doesn't know how to live in the moment and enjoy what she has. She's grown so accustomed to striving for more that she doesn't know what to do now that she has arrived. Her life has always been about the pursuit of her next goal and she's having a tough time changing the way she's lived for so many years. Bridget is still on medication today and has yet to feel that she can come off of it. She was making progress in therapy but took six months off last year and is now just getting back to her weekly sessions. Unfortunately, I cannot check Bridget off as a success story just yet, but the year is young.

Another good friend of mine who shared his story with me was Dan—the laid back, happy, calm person in our group of friends. I never saw someone roll with the punches as well as Dan did. If you told him his car was stolen, he'd pause for five seconds, wince, then ask if you wanted to grab a burger on the way to the police station to file a report. Well, Dan began experiencing panic attacks during his freshman year of college. His first attack came a few weeks into his first semester and he had no idea what it was. The feelings and symptoms had surprised him so much that he had to go to the infirmary. They continued for weeks and even months and he could not understand why they were happening. He began to see a psychiatrist on a weekly basis. Within a few months he got his attacks under control and realized that he was subconsciously panicking and stressing over his new independent life. His move to college and his change in lifestyle triggered his fear of growing up and leaving home.

To this day Dan has not shared his experience with anyone but me. All of us who knew him then never knew that he was dealing with these issues. Like me, Dan hid his struggle, went to class everyday, and socialized as best he could. He only shared this story with me when I confided in him about my own struggle with anxiety. His story was one of the first that I heard. It comforted me greatly and gave me my first glimpse of hope.

Dan also shared with me a story about his mother. She was in a car accident a few years back and lost the eyesight in her left eye. She was an avid tennis player and golfer and this injury kept her from playing ever again. The loss of eyesight soon became her only focus and she began to experience anxiety and depression. This life changing injury altered the way she viewed herself and the way she had once lived her life. Essentially it altered her view of happiness. She began to speak with a therapist who put her on Zoloft. Six weeks later she began to feel better. When I first started taking Zoloft I was hoping to feel better very quickly and when I didn't, I got frustrated. It was this insight from Dan's mother's experience that gave me the understanding and knowledge to patiently wait for my symptoms to subside. And in roughly six weeks they did.

Today, Dan's mother is off of her medication and happy and healthy. She no longer plays tennis or golf but has found interest in many other activities, including gardening, jogging, and chess. Through therapy she came to the realization that she had two choices—one, sulk and continue to be depressed that this unfortunate accident happened to her, or two, accept this life altering accident as a challenge and an opportunity to explore what else life may have to offer. I'm sure she misses her tennis and golf outings, but today, she chooses not to focus on what she's missing but rather on what she's found. She no longer views her accident as a tragedy, but rather as a motivator and an opportunity to branch out and find new interests.

It's obvious that all of these people have one thing in common, and that's anxiety. Most of the causes of their anxiety differ and many of these people differ, but anxiety is the common thread. This was no different with my good friend, Mike, a very successful businessman. He's been with the same firm for almost seven years and has made his way up to senior manager at the age of twenty-nine. He has done this ahead of all of his peers. Mike is motivated, intelligent, accountable and trustworthy. He makes a good friend and a great manager. Two years ago, Mike met his girlfriend of eight years for dinner in Boston after work. They had been together since college and loved each other very much, or so we all thought. Mike had been waiting for her to graduate from law school before proposing and at that point her graduation was just five weeks away. When he met her at the restaurant he noticed she didn't look like her usual self. She was visibly upset and uncomfortable. She broke up with Mike. She told him that even though she loved him dearly, she didn't think they were right for each other.

As you can imagine, Mike was devastated. He tried to pull himself together and go about his job and life as if things were alright, but inside Mike was dying. He began experiencing anxiety attacks all the time. Many times he would lose his ability to breathe and begin to hyperventilate. This would happen at work, at his desk, at home, even in his car. Not only did these attacks take over his life, but they were also driving him into depression. He was depressed about losing his girlfriend, but soon became even more depressed for having to struggle each day with such anxiety. His depression slowly took over and he eventually began to lie in his bed until early afternoon, dreading going to work. He lost interest in many things including his love for traveling. At the height of his anxiety and depression he just didn't feel like being away from home. Traveling became a nuisance and a challenge. A few weeks later, Mike sought professional help.

Within time Mike was able to understand why he started having his attacks and he slowly began to get them under control. Today, Mike is doing well. He has yet to find a new love but lives believing that everything happens for a reason. Rather than focus on missing his ex-girlfriend and all that was good about their relationship, Mike has become a realist. He had always known that there were things about their relationship that were problematic, yet his feelings of love caused him to overlook those things. Today, he gently acknowledges his continued affection for his ex-girlfriend but focuses more on the fact that they weren't right for each other. Their differences would have made for a challenging life together. Now Mike knows exactly what he wants and needs. His time in therapy gave him a much better understanding of himself and he is patiently waiting for someone who will one day compliment him.

The last story that I'll share with you is about a coworker named Liz. I have been colleagues with Liz for almost seven years now and we have developed a great friendship on top of a very good working relationship. Liz has been married for fifteen years and has one son, Jack; a five-year-old and Liz's pride and joy. He was not an easy child to conceive. Liz and her husband spent three years trying and actually had to use in vitro fertilization in order to bring Jack into this world. They were successful on their third attempt.

Liz is a very caring and nurturing mother and would do anything for her family. She has always dreamed of having a big family and has been trying to conceive another child for the past two years. All of her attempts have been unsuccessful. Her husband has given up hope and is happy with only Jack but she yearns for at least one more child.

Just recently Liz began experiencing anxiety. She hasn't had any severe attacks but can experience an hour at a time when her mind continually races and she becomes dizzy, off-balance, and confused. These episodes happen a few times a week and are only part of her struggle with anxiety. She hasn't slept well and hasn't had much of an appetite for months. Her motivation and interest in daily activities has slowly dwindled and she can't seem to find happiness. Four weeks ago she finally decided to go see a therapist. She's been seeing him each week since.

Although it is early in her treatments, Liz has been making progress. Therapy has begun to show Liz where her mind has gone awry. Most of her issues have stemmed from her inability to conceive another child and she once told me that this has been the hardest thing she has ever had to accept. She is used to working hard at something and coming out with positive results. Liz's strong work ethic, the same one that has propelled her to the top of her professional field, has also hindered her acceptance of her inability to conceive. She wants another child so badly that she can't think about anything else. Rather than see the blessing that she has in front of her in Jack, along with a loving husband and many other fortunes, she struggles with what she doesn't have. Her unsuccessful attempts to produce a sibling for Jack have derailed her life and her happiness. Thankfully, she now understands how she needs to change her focus and where she needs to guide her thoughts and energy. After months of turmoil she is on the right path.

It's important to note that all of these people are intelligent, caring, and hard-working. They have also all had some type of anxiety disorder and many of them had experienced depression. Although the causes of their anxiety all differ it's important to realize that their struggles, their symptoms, and their roads to recovery share many similarities. The most important similarity being that they all decided to seek professional help. As a country, we are extremely fortunate to have therapy readily available at our fingertips, many times even covered by our insurance plans. Additionally, we are lucky to live in a time when the medical field has made many amazing discoveries and break-throughs in the fields of anxiety and depression. Today's therapy offers very sophisticated behavioral techniques, informative mind and body skills, and many new and non-addicting medications. Previous generations weren't as fortunate to benefit from the great medical technology that we enjoy today.

As I was thinking about the fortunes of our generation, I spoke to my mother on the phone. We talked about some of the stories and struggles of others and she started to tell me about her Aunt Marge, her father's sister. I am not sure why she never told me about this aunt before but it was the first I had ever heard of her. My mother went on to tell me that her aunt had had a nervous breakdown back in the mid-1950s while she was in her early thirties. Soon thereafter she was committed to a home and lived most of her life under intense supervision. Because of this, my mother never got to see her Aunt Marge again but always remembered her aunt's fate.

Obviously, society has made strides since then and we are lucky to have the knowledge, therapy, and medications that are available today. The development of science has increased our understanding of how our mind and body work together. It has also illustrated how serotonin and other chemicals can create imbalances in the brain. Today, not only do we have science on our side, we also have fifty additional years of research, tests, and results that have made professional therapy what it is today. Therapists have spent years learning from each other and sharing successful treatments. After speaking with my mother, I felt especially thankful that we live in the time in which we do. Fifty years ago, the lack of knowledge and treatments may have led some of us to a fate much like my Great Aunt Marge! She never had the opportunity to learn, recover, and live a fruitful and happy life. Chances are she had a quarter-life crisis before it was ever even diagnosed.

14

Today—Standing Up Again

My interest in writing this book stemmed from my desire to help people, especially those who share my issues with anxiety. Also, I feel that it's extremely important to inform others about anxiety and anxiety disorders because there is still very little knowledge about the topic today. How can we be expected to deal with anxiety if we never learn about its symptoms, causes, effects, and the techniques and strategies needed to overcome the condition? How will we learn to live healthy, balanced, happy lives?

Information regarding anxiety and depression should even be taught to kids in high school and college to prepare our younger generations. As the future leaders of tomorrow, they deserve to be equipped with the skills needed to succeed in life. Rather than let them experience anxiety the way I was forced to, let's be proactive and equip them with the knowledge and skills needed to combat anxiety. That way, they can be knowledgeable and avoid anxiety's harmful effects instead of reacting to them blindly.

We teach health education in high school. We do this because it's important that teens understand how the human body works. Through this forum they learn how to respect and care for their bodies and keep it safe from disease. Aren't anxiety disorders and depression a similar threat? Shouldn't we teach our children how to avoid such disorders in order to give them a fighting chance? The answer is simple—yes!

Today I live anxiety and depression free. I am completely off of medication and am extremely happy. I am thankful for my journey and now spend my time focusing on my new set of goals. I wake up everyday and enjoy my warm shower, my morning coffee, and my commute to work listening to the radio or reading the paper. I no longer dread going to work. I look forward to the day at hand and I don't worry about what's in store for me tomorrow or further down the road. I don't agonize about when I will need to "grow up", or if I will get married and have a family. I feel content and extremely fortunate to be where I am today. I simply focus on the tasks and enjoyments of each day. Living for today has never had the clarity that it does now.

In looking back at what I went through, I am amazed by some of the thoughts and feelings I once had. Today, I finally see where I went wrong—I fixated on my concerns about future life experiences that weren't even close to my reality at that time. I allowed those thoughts to control me to the point where they became extremely detrimental. Some of those concerns seem silly to me today but I will never forget the way they made me feel back then. My anxiety, and my subsequent anger and disgust at not being able to control that anxiety, were all very real. And of course my lack of knowledge about anxiety only increased the magnitude of my terrible feelings. If I had had the awareness and ability to identify my negative thoughts, and then change and control them, I feel that I would have avoided my anxiety disorder altogether. Because of my lack of knowledge, I allowed my thoughts and feelings to create a world of anxiety for me. This became habitual and soon my negative thoughts ruled my life.

When I was seven years old, I was stung by a bumblebee in my backyard while swimming in my pool one August afternoon. It had been a rather terrifying experience. So much so in fact that I remember thinking to myself how awful it was that bees even existed and how much happier I'd be if they didn't. After that bee sting, I developed a fear of bees for weeks. I didn't want to go swimming or play outside anymore. My fear of being stung took away all of the enjoyment those gorgeous summer days had to offer. My irrational wish for bumblebees to disappear from this earth was so strong that it is still vivid in my mind today. And just a few months ago, I had the same feeling about anxiety—I wished it never existed. I dreamed about a perfect world. This time, a world without anxiety disorders instead of bumblebees. Yet I knew it was an impossible wish. That type of anxiety-free utopia doesn't exist. In addition, I wouldn't want it to. Anxiety, like bumblebees, plays an important role in human nature and in our society as a whole. So, just as I did with my fear of bumblebees, I accepted anxiety as a necessary part of life—one that I would soon learn to live with and manage.

Over the past year I have learned more than I ever thought I would about anxiety. In fact, I began learning so much I had to start writing things down, hence this book and my cheat sheet. But this knowledge and my development with these skills took time. You have to practice such skills, and most importantly, be patient with yourself. It's like riding a bicycle. First it takes someone to initially show you how to ride, and then it takes time and practice from you. Learning something new typically doesn't happen overnight. Time and practice will enable you to reach your destination, guaranteed.

It's also important to understand that the road to recovery can be full of peaks and valleys. Just when you think you have turned the corner, you might have a bad day and feel like you're back at square one, full of anxiety and frustration. The key is not to let a down day get you down and keep you down. One bad day tends to seem a lot worse when you are going through an anxiety disorder, but try to take it for what it is—simply a bad day. Realize that everyone has a bad day now and again. Most importantly, have the ability to bounce back after such a day—don't carry that bad day into the next!

As you get better at bouncing back from minor setbacks, you will begin to experience less of them. Before you know it, there will be more ups than downs. Also, the anxiety-avoidance skills you've spent time practicing will start to become second nature to you. You won't need to consciously try to control your mind as much anymore. Things *will* get better.

I have always taken for granted being happy, living anxiety free, and living a life full of success, triumph, and enjoyment. It wasn't until I hit this bump in the road that I began to realize happiness and contentment are not givens, they are gifts. Better yet, they are gifts that you sometimes need to work for. Life is about ups and downs and it's not what happens to you, it's how you interpret and handle what happens to you that is most important. About ten years ago I was given some great advice that I never truly appreciated until this year. My sister told me to "enjoy the good times and weather the bad." It's this advice that ten years later means more to me than ever before. Over the past year I've learned to appreciate the good times much much more while managing through the bad. I've realized that the bad times will eventually pass and it's just a matter of getting through them, weathering them, that counts. Just like a storm that rolls through a beach town—you have to board up the windows and batten down the hatches until it passes and the sun comes out once again.

I am living proof that you can conquer your anxiety disorder. I've heard many people ask the question: *Can you fully recover from anxiety?* And I've heard just as many different answers. My opinion is that you *can* fully recover from an *anxiety disorder.* You can overcome a disorder which limits your life—your activities and your happiness—and eventually get back to enjoying your life. But I don't think anxious people can overcome or fully recover from anxiety itself. As you know, anxiety is a natural emotion and a part of human beings. It's not something you can rid your body of, nor would you want to. When under control anxiety can be a very positive trait. The key is to manage anxiety so it remains at a healthy and positive level.

Janet Fronk once explained to me that anxiety is, and always has been, present within all of us. It doesn't simply appear or come on all of a sudden. It is only when you recognize this anxiety that you begin to focus on it, especially if your experiences happen to be dreadful ones. She compared it to a diagnosed disorder called *Tinnitus*. People with Tinnitus hear continuous ringing in their ears, day in and day out. It becomes so burdensome and distracting that these people have a tough time focusing on anything other than the ringing in their ears. The interesting thing about this is that we all can hear ringing if we listen for it. It's not something that just appears one day. It's there if we choose to look for it and focus on it—just like anxiety. In both situations, it's a matter of how we interpret and perceive things. When we view anxiety as a negative, we begin to focus on it with the intention of correcting it, and at that point we give the condition life! Harping on anxiety allows it to fester and grow. With patience and practice you can train your mind to no longer focus on your anxiety and pay more attention to other aspects of your life. Moving forward does not involve ridding your mind and body of anxiety entirely; it involves learning how to control it and then let it be.

Just like life, recovery is not a destination, but rather a journey. As each day passes I am committed to my recovery and I've continued to make great progress. But progress requires continued practice and effort. It takes practice to keep your mind sharp and effort to embed the anti-anxiety skills into your everyday thought process. Soon the practice and effort you put into mastering these skills will seem less like practice and more like part of you. That is when you can say that you have changed! At that point some might even say that you've *recovered*—for your battle with anxiety will be fought naturally rather than with a deliberate and conscious effort.

I want to leave you with an illustration on how your mind will one day operate once you've thoroughly committed and practiced the anti-anxiety skills described in this book. Have you ever driven home with something else on your mind and found yourself pulling into your driveway with minimal recollection of the actual drive? I sure have—all the time in fact. So imagine moving to a new city and a new home, a place that you have never been before. The first week you'd probably have to follow written directions in order to find your way to the mall, to the drug store, or even your way home from work. Perhaps you even spoke to a few different people and investigated alternative routes to figure out what was the best way. Going home each night you'd have to pay close attention to every turn and stop sign. You'd take a few wrong turns here or there before learning from your mistakes. You might even get lost? As time went on, you'd slowly stop making mistakes. With every potential wrong turn you'd be able to correct yourself sooner because you'd immediately realize that you made a mistake. Soon after that you would no longer make any wrong turns; you'd be able to stop yourself before you even put on your blinker. Your mind became trained to identify wrong turns based on your previous experiences. As time went on your drive home would become second nature to you and you'd be able to do it subconsciously.

Once you garner the skills discussed in this book you will soon find the right path without much effort. Your trained mind will lead you in the right direction with minimal thought. Your daily drive will soon become automated and enjoyable. No longer will you need to worry about making a wrong turn, your experiences and knowledge will get you home. Similar to how your anti-anxiety skills will lead you in the right direction once you hone them as your own. It's here that it's no longer considered practice or effort but rather your own natural thoughts and reactions. It's also here that the road of life will become much clearer to you. So drive safely!

The Cheat Sheet

- ❖ Breathe, relax, and slow down
- ❖ TODAY – Live for today and be present
- ❖ Stop future thinking – don't get bogged down with 'what ifs' and 'shoulds'
- ❖ Identify and control your negative thinking
- ❖ Be happy in spite of problems – things will not be perfect for life is not perfect, there is no blueprint to follow
- ❖ Be thankful for your health and the moments you are fortunate enough to live (Sonny)
- ❖ Don't be so hard on yourself
- ❖ Accept your feelings and don't anticipate how you will feel
- ❖ Put it into perspective—don't let anxiety become your main focus
- ❖ Have courage—bring it on!
- ❖ Be happy with progress and know that this will pass
- ❖ Better for going through this
- ❖ Maximize the positives—turn negatives into positives
- ❖ Anxiety will become less captive and scary
- ❖ Be comfortable with yourself wherever you are